WHAT NEXT

Designing a Life of Purpose and Clarity

Raghavendra Mithare lives in London with his wife and daughter. A computer science engineer by training and a passionate professional coach (PCC from ICF) by calling, he is committed to helping people live lives of clarity and purpose. Drawing on over two decades of experience in the technology and transformation space—as well as his lifelong dedication to personal growth—Raghav/Ragz has supported leaders across industries to unlock their potential and design more meaningful futures. WHAT NEXT is his first book, a self-published labour of love created entirely by hand—from writing to cover design and layout.

(c) 2025, Raghavendra Mithare, All rights reserved.
Cover Design Artwork : Nishka Mithare

ISBN : 978 - 1 - 0684198 - 0 - 5

Edition 1 / 002

"In life you wind up with one of two things - the results or the reason why you don't have the results. Results don't have to be explained. They just are."- **Werner Erhard**

WHAT

DESIGNING A LIFE OF

NEXT

PURPOSE AND CLARITY

RAGHAVENDRA MITHARE, PCC

Bystander Publication
ISBN: 9781068419805

Copyright Notice & Acknowledgment

Copyright © 2025 by Raghavendra Mithare

All rights reserved. No part of this book may be reproduced, distributed, or transmitted in any form or by any means, including photocopying, recording, or other electronic or mechanical methods, without prior written permission from the author, except in the case of brief quotations embodied in critical reviews, academic references, or educational purposes under fair use doctrine. For permissions, contact: mithare@explorewhatnext.com.

Acknowledgment of Third-Party Works

This book references concepts, frameworks, and quotations from various authors, philosophers, researchers, and business leaders. While every effort has been made to provide proper attribution, the following key works and influences are acknowledged: The Hero's Journey™ – Concept by Joseph Campbell, referenced for its application in personal transformation.

The Kübler-Ross Grief Curve™ – Developed by Elisabeth Kübler-Ross, used to explain human response to change. Ikigai: The Japanese Philosophy of a Meaningful Life – Acknowledgment of the concept originating from Japanese culture and referenced in works by Héctor García and Francesc Miralles. Mindset: The New Psychology of Success™ – Concept introduced by Carol Dweck. Getting Things Done® (GTD®) – Productivity methodology by David Allen.Think and Grow Rich® – Principles based on Napoleon Hill's work. Landmark Forum® & Ontological Leadership – Acknowledgment of Werner Erhard's influence on transformational coaching.

References to AI & Technology – Concepts related to OpenAI's GPT-3™/GPT-4™, DeepMind's AlphaFold®, Google Knowledge Graph™, and other AI-related frameworks. The above frameworks and ideas are used for educational and illustrative purposes. Any direct quotes have been attributed to their original sources.

Trademark Notice & Disclaimer

The following trademarks are referenced in this book: Google®, Apple®, Microsoft®, IBM®, Amazon®, Alibaba®, Tesla®, OpenAI™, DeepMind®, Pixar®, GPT-3™, GPT-4™, AlphaFold®, Tata Group®, Rocky®, Star Wars®, The Matrix®, and others.

All trademarks, product names, company names, and logos appearing in this book are the property of their respective owners. The use of these names is for reference only and does not imply any affiliation, sponsorship, endorsement, or partnership.

Fair Use & Educational Use Disclaimer

This book includes references, short excerpts, and discussions of widely known frameworks, theories, and case studies for educational, illustrative, and transformative purposes. These references fall under fair use as they are used for commentary, criticism, research, and education.

If any content owner believes their work has been used inappropriately, please contact the author at mithare@explorewhatnext.com to address concerns and provide proper attribution if required.

Early Praise for WHAT NEXT – Designing a Life of Purpose and Clarity

"Brilliant!"
Paul Darnall,
FOUNDER, 3S KNOWLEDGE SOLUTIONS, WARWICK, UK

"As a coach, I often meet clients at a crossroads—navigating mid-life transitions and searching for deeper meaning—who ask, 'What next?' Raghavendra Mithare masterfully offers a roadmap that is both structured and deeply personal, guiding readers from uncertainty to clarity. WHAT NEXT is a powerful companion for transformation, and I highly recommend it to coaches, mentors, and leaders who wish to gift their clients a meaningful tool to help them design the life they truly deserve."
Bhaskar Natarajan,
MCC (ICF), EXECUTIVE, LEADERSHIP AND CXO COACH, BENGALURU, INDIA

"What Next is an eye-opening book in which Raghav chronicles his lifelong journey, crafting a masterful and refreshing guide to building a life of purpose and fulfilment."
Rajkumar Noubade, PhD
DIRECTOR, ONCOLOGY RESEARCH AT GILEAD SCIENCES INC., FOSTER CITY, CA, USA

"A friendly guide for anyone looking for clarity and purpose. It makes you think!"
Manjunath Doddamani,
IT LEADER, PUNE, INDIA

"A must-have for anyone who wants to be better."
Sven Ihnken,
BUSINESS COACH, LONDON, UK

"Well done! This is a powerful guide for anyone looking for clarity and direction."
Ravindra Kullarni,
SCHOOL FRIEND, LEADER IN MNC, BENGALURU, INDIA

"Designing a Life of Purpose and Clarity is a deeply human book. It's personal, and it reflects Ragz's integrity, warmth, and humility. I found it both moving and inspiring."
Michel Crook,
AGILE COACH / MINDFULNESS COACH, BIRMINGHAM, UK

"In the silence that follows a life-altering setback, WHAT NEXT finds its voice. Like sitting with a friend who has weathered the storm, it's a soulful tribute to courage, vulnerability, and the strength to begin again — one that lingers long after the final page."
Rajeev K. S.,
SENIOR IT LEADER AT FORTUNE 500 COMPANY, USA

"GQC presents a well-structured, articulate framework for goal-setting — one that resonates with professionals at various stages of their journey. Insightful, grounded, and practical, this book is a valuable read for anyone navigating growth, challenges, or transitions in their career."
Kumarswamy Sulikere,
PROGRAMME MANAGER AT TCS, NETHERLANDS

"WHAT NEXT is a wonderful read. It offers clear guidance for self-discovery, helping you gain clarity of thought and a strong sense of direction to take meaningful action."
Shrikant Halanayak,
SENIOR DATA ENGINEER, BP AUSTRALIA, MELBOURNE

"From finding yourself lost in the undergrounds of life to putting yourself back in the zone! It's a must-read for anyone ready to get back on track."
Divya Sareen,
PROFESSIONAL SCRUM MASTER, HCL TECH, GERMANY

"Wow — congratulations, Raghav! And thank you so much for sharing your first book. What truly resonated with me was this line: 'Authenticity is the most powerful way to live, operate, and express ourselves — it's the ultimate and most natural filter for everything.'"
Savitha SR,
COGNITIVE FITNESS COACH, BENGALURU, INDIA

"Purpose without clarity is a modern-day tragedy. Raghav offers practical tools and techniques for meaningful self-reflection and empowers you to develop your own roadmap to success."
Deepak Malhotra,
PARTNER, INFOSYS CONSULTING, UK

"I know Raghav since the last 5 years as he has played a very critical role in my coaching journey while I was still undergoing coach training . I find him extremely patient, emphathetic listener and a coach with a growth mindset His presence makes everyone feel comfortable in terms of opening up and sharing fearlessly. In his training programs that I attended, he exudes confidence and provides an environment of calmness, learning with an open mind and bringing clarity of the subject. He does not stop at providing the right training inputs , he goes the extra mile to see you through execution of training goals. He is truly an asset to any one who would like you create a competitive advantage through learning and development."
Arijit Mitra,
SENIOR DIRECTOR BUSINESS DEVELOPMENT AT THE AFRICA OPERATING UNIT ,COCA -COLA COMPANY.

"The privilege of a lifetime is to become who you truly are."

– Carl Jung

To

my parents **Malathi Mithare and Dr Mohan Mithare**

To

my **wife,** **Veena,**
and our daughter
Nishka

To

Swami Sarvapriyanda

To

Werner Erhard

Preface

I wrote the first draft of this book in just 14 days—motivated by a personal challenge and inspired by Sylvester Stallone, who famously wrote Rocky in four. Although the writing itself was fast, the ideas behind it come from over 20 years of experience—drawn from articles, blog posts, coaching sessions, and personal reflections.

The real reason I started writing wasn't ambition—it was frustration. I had lost my job, faced repeated rejections in interviews, and began questioning everything. Writing this book made me think deeply and reflect honestly. It was an emotional journey and also a healing process. I may or may not write another book—that's why you might see many dedications and a long list of acknowledgements.

I simply wanted to say 'Thank you' to everyone who supported me during difficult times. As human beings, we have a powerful ability to support and heal one another.

One of the thoughts that sparked my journey as a creator and writer came from reflecting on the nature of life. I was on a long walk one winter morning when it hit me: "In the end, nothing really matters—you won't take your money or fame with you when you die." But then another thought followed: "What you do take with you is your knowledge, experiences, and unique perspectives." That moment shifted something in me. I realised it's not enough to only consume content—we must also create. Read, yes—but also write. Learn—but also share and teach.

If this book helps even one person gain clarity, feel hopeful, or take a step toward their purpose (possibly publish a book), then it has done its job.

I chose to self-publish this book so I wouldn't have to depend on agencies. At first, I thought writing the draft would be the hardest part—but I soon realised that publishing a book involves much more: editing, proofreading, formatting, and designing the cover. To refine the writing, I used tools like Grammarly, ChatGPT, Hemingway Editor, and ProWritingAid. I also felt like this was a team effort—many people helped review and proofread the manuscript and early drafts. The most challenging part was learning Adobe InDesign—it's a powerful and beautiful tool, but it took a lot of time just to grasp the basics. Still, I managed to learn enough to format this book myself.

This book is entirely self-published—from the research and writing to the cover design, editing, and formatting. As a perfectionist, I know there's always room for improvement. But as the saying goes, "Version One is better than Version None." Unlike software, a printed book can't be patched or updated once it's on the shelf—there's no second release.

While I've tried my best to ensure accuracy, some mistakes may have slipped through. If you come across any, please do share them with me—I'd be grateful for the chance to learn and improve.

What You'll Find Inside This Book

Part I: Foundation – The Inner Work

Focuses on self-discovery, purpose, and mindset. Learn how to align your values with your goals, redefine success, and build resilience.

Part II: Navigating Life's Vectors

Explores strategic thinking tools like Vector Thinking and the Life Design Canvas to help you find direction and balance in life.

Part III: Resources & Challenges in Transformation

This section tackles common challenges such as time, money, and limiting beliefs. Learn practical tools for productivity, financial health, and how language shapes your reality.

Part IV: Execution & Next Steps

The final section explores how to keep going when things get hard. Discover how to stay motivated, navigate an AI-driven world, and practise Ganbatte—the Japanese idea of doing your best. The final chapter, WHAT NEXT, is a call to action for living with purpose and possibility.

Annexures

Deepen your learning with helpful tools like the Kübler-Ross Grief Curve, the Hero's Journey, Ikigai, and Ontology—the study of being.

Hope you enjoy reading this book.

Raghavendra Mithare

Table of Contents

Part I: Foundation – The Inner Work

Choices That Define You	3
Your Hero's Journey: The Path to Reinvention	13
Purpose and Meaning: Finding Your True North	20

Part II: Clearing the Roadblocks

Time–It Is About You	35
Money: Its History, Psychology, and Mindset	46
Redesigning Relationships	62

Part III: Designing a Life You Love

Designing a Life of Purpose and Meaning	76
The GQC Framework: Rethinking Goals	87
Vector Thinking: Aligning Speed & Direction	98

Part IV: Keeping The Momentum

Navigating Uncertainty: AI and You	109
Happiness: The True Measure of Success	118
Ganbatte - Do Your Best, Keep Going	127
WHAT NEXT – Final Thoughts	136

Annexures (Reference Material)

The Kübler-Ross Grief Curve	151
The Hero's Journey	159
Ikigai	164
Ontology	171

Closing

Acknowledgements	179
My Journey	186

Part I: Foundation – The Inner Work

Build awareness, rediscover your story, and reconnect with your purpose.

"In the middle of every difficulty lies opportunity."
— *Albert Einstein*

CHAPTER 1

Choices That Define You

A lot of people go through life without much thought. Their destiny is determined by their reactions to events, rather than their actions. This book helps you seize control of your destiny. It covers your career, relationships, personal growth, and achievements. Break free from feeling stuck with the help of this guide. Get ready to feel inspired and immediately implement changes right away. It shifts your view and removes the need to wait for the perfect moment.

When life feels stagnant—if frustration, fear, or stress weigh you down—you're not alone. A minor victory might bring a fleeting high, but soon, the same sense of being trapped returns. I know this experience well—because I've lived it.

But here's the truth: you don't have to stay stuck. Change begins the moment you accept your situation and decide to move forward. With the right mindset, tools, and actions, you can break free and create a life of purpose, growth, and fulfillment. For several years, I was going through the motions. I made a major move from Bangalore to London to establish the ProcessWhirl in the UK. The company we built with passion but had to shut down during COVID-19. My unprocessed disappointment over closing ProcessWhirl was one reason for feeling stuck.

Despite the challenges, Kishore—the founder—and I ensured that none of our staff left stranded. We helped them secure jobs elsewhere before shutting down the company. On top of that, we often underestimate how hard it is to settle in a new country, especially in mid-life.

After that, I joined a major oil and gas company, eager to contribute my knowledge and skills. Though relieved to have a job, my ego surfaced when I realised the position was at a level I had performed earlier. I tried to push those feelings aside. But they kept resurfacing—especially when I was made to sit through training I had once delivered or when I was overlooked for challenging assignments.

In hindsight, the line between self-respect and pride is thin—only we can determine where it lies.

After a year and a half, I realised I hadn't earned the leadership team's confidence, and growth opportunities felt nonexistent. Fortunately, I secured a better opportunity with a wealth management company—double the salary and a promising position. At first, everything seemed great, but soon, challenges surfaced. While I built trust and gained respect from most of the team, aligning with one senior stakeholder proved difficult. Their leadership style—rooted in authority and control—clashed with my approach. It was unlike anything I had encountered before.

As someone known for managing stakeholders and navigating complex relationships, this experience made me question my own abilities. The challenge, shaped by multiple factors, left a lasting impact—but it also deepened my understanding of leadership dynamics.

A few months later, a merger led to downsizing, and I lost my job. While I felt relieved to leave behind the stress, the uncertainty of being without an income was overwhelming—especially after just purchasing a home with a substantial mortgage.

Things progressed, as my wife was employed. I grounded myself in a simple truth: our basic needs—food, shelter, and warmth—were secure. At first, I put on a brave face, often saying, 'When life throws lemons, don't just make lemonade—see if you can make a cocktail and add more value.', but when reality set in, I spiralled downward.

I received a diagnosis of mild depression at my lowest point. Even in that struggle, I glimpsed the profound battle faced by those grappling with clinical depression. At times, I felt lost. But with the support of counsellors and Cognitive Behavioural Therapy (CBT), family and friends, I got back my peace. This experience reshaped my understanding of human needs. Having met our necessities, we seek connection and purpose.

In hindsight, that period became one of the greatest opportunities for self-discovery. It deepened my empathy for mental health challenges and gave me a renewed sense of purpose. My observation is people avoid discussing mental health due to the stigma attached to it. As per the NHS, One in 4 people experience some form of mental health challenge every year. I learned that while most people want to help, they hesitate—afraid of intruding. Meanwhile, the person struggling will not be able to ask for support. Most people go through mental health challenges considering it as part of life. A good support structure might minimise the impact. It can also avoid the person slipping into more serious conditions.

It's a difficult gap to bridge, but perhaps instead of waiting for someone to reach out, we should take the first step—by showing our own vulnerability and acknowledging our limitations. I realised this is easier said than done, and I still have much to learn about mental health support and advocacy. But what I understand is that minor acts of kindness and care can make a world of difference.

I am grateful for the unwavering help of my family, friends, and fellow coaches. Their presence reminded me I wasn't alone. Going out in nature, taking long walks, reading, and photography helped me a lot. My spiritual practices also became a pillar of strength and guiding me through my recovery and helping me find clarity and purpose amidst the chaos.

The real shift came when a friend invited me to collaborate on designing a workshop. The creative engagement, coupled with financial compensation, reignited my confidence. I realised that money isn't just a measure of value—it's a tangible recognition of contribution. This period taught me both the power and the limitations of money.

I resumed coaching engagements, and with each session, my spirits lifted. Yet, I kept applying for jobs—over 200 applications. Each rejection, no matter how politely phrased, felt like reopening an old wound. The worst part? Hours of preparation for interviews, only to face being turned away—or worse, silence. I'm still learning to navigate rejection, but now I channel that energy into creativity. Writing this book became one such experiment.

As my wife was working, we had our basic needs for safety and security met. But I felt a deep emptiness—as if life were slipping through my fingers. A growing desperation took hold, fuelling a restless search for meaning.

The turning point came when two of my childhood pals who now live in the U.S. visited. Another childhood friend who lives locally joined us. We had an enjoyable time, reminding me of the good old times. My buddies were mindful of my financial situation, but I had budgeted carefully, ensuring we could create meaningful experiences without overspending.

One friend stayed behind for a couple of days to support me. We explored London and had deep conversations that offered much-needed perspectives. That's when I came across an ad for the MJ Musical. I found the tickets reasonably priced, so I booked them. In retrospect, I now see that decision as a pivotal moment in shaping my future.

The show was breathtaking. As it unfolded, I felt a profound internal shift. Just as Gautama Buddha attained nirvana under the Bodhi tree (though I didn't reach nirvana!), something clicked inside me during the MJ Musical—I was no longer the same person.

At that instant, I reconnected with my purpose and inspiration. For me, it was my Just Beat It moment. As Tony

Robbins says: 'Your destiny is shaped in your moments of decision.'

This experience reminded me of a story that has shaped my perspective on life. I first came across it during my school days, and it has guided me ever since:

The Story of Eagle and the Chickens

A man walking through a forest found a young eagle. He took it home and placed it in his barnyard, where it soon learned to eat chicken feed and behave like a chicken.

One day, a naturalist passing by asked why an eagle—the king of birds—was living among chickens.

"Since I have given it chicken feed and trained it to be a chicken, it has never learned to fly," the owner replied. "It behaves like a chicken, so it is no longer an eagle."

"Still," insisted the naturalist, "it has the heart of an eagle and it surely can learn to fly."

Determined to prove this, the naturalist took the eagle in his arms and said, "You belong to the sky, not the earth. Stretch forth your wings and fly."

The eagle hesitated, glancing at the chickens pecking at their food. Then, it jumped down to join them.

Undeterred, the naturalist took the eagle to the roof and urged it again: "You are an eagle! Stretch forth your wings and fly." But, afraid of the unknown, the eagle returned to the barnyard.

On the third day, the naturalist took the eagle to a high mountain. Holding the bird high, he encouraged it once more:

"You are an eagle. You belong to the sky. Stretch forth your wings and fly."

The eagle hesitated. But then, as it looked up at the sun, something awakened within. Slowly, it stretched its wings. Then, with a triumphant cry, it soared into the heavens.

This story left a lasting impact on me. It inspired me to explore my potential through learning and experimentation. More importantly, it deepened my passion for helping others uncover who they truly are.

Reconnecting with my purpose changed my perspective. A pivotal moment was attending a Digital Public Infrastructure session where I met Aadhar's architect, Pramod Verma. I'm inspired by his Aadhaar creation story. It focuses on addressing large-scale societal challenges. His philosophy centers on small-scale experimentation and problem simplification via unbundling. When I applied these principles in my situation, I came to understand that All I was dealing with was 'anticipated problems' and the rest were 'concerns' that everyone will have. That winter night, on my walk back from the session, the realisation hit me: we can make a difference in people's lives without needing permission.

You might start something small as long as it at least makes you happy. What is more important, is it to prove how good you are? or Creating a journey of purpose and fulfillment that makes you satisfied and content? That is when I decided to teach, write, and share. Help others in whatever way I can. To nudge people to explore their full potential.

Every moment presents a choice. You can stay where you are—waiting, hesitating, hoping for the perfect moment—or you can take a step forward.

Unlocking Your True Potential – Awareness, Action and Adaptability

Every transformation begins with a choice. The first stage is Awareness—recognising when you're stuck, feeling unfulfilled, or trapped in patterns that no longer serve you. Too often, we wait for the 'perfect moment' that never comes. The next pillar is Action—taking that first, often uncomfortable, step forward despite fear, doubt, or uncertainty. Progress is never about waiting; it's about moving. Finally, Adaptability allows us to embrace change as growth, understanding that setbacks are not failures but stepping stones.

Aligning awareness, action, and adaptability reclaims your power, redefines your future, and allows you to step into a life of purpose and possibility.

The choice to soar or stay grounded is yours. Don't settle. Don't wait for permission. Take the risk, make the move, and accept the risk of failure. As you take up any journey, failures are part of the game. You can consider failures as feedback so you improve and move on.

Failure isn't the end—it's proof that you tried, that you dared to step beyond comfort. The only real failure is standing still, not taking any action towards your goal. Like the eagle, we all possess immense potential—we just need to unlock it.

My vision is to inspire others to find their true potential. I want to help them create a life full of possibilities. I will keep exploring my potential. I'm committed to building a community of people who want to explore their potential and contribute to each other and the society at large.

Mission: To serve others.

Questions for Reflection

- *Are you living on autopilot, or are you actively shaping your future?*

- *What past setbacks or disappointments have you yet to fully process, and how might they be holding you back?*

- *Where in your life are you mistaking ego for self-respect? How can you redefine that boundary?*

- *What small decision could you make today that might become a turning point in your journey?*

- *What beliefs about yourself are limiting your potential, and how can you challenge them?*

References and further reading

James, Muriel, and Dorothy Jongeward. Born to Win: Transactional Analysis with Gestalt Experiments. Addison-Wesley, 1971.

Covey, Stephen R. The 7 Habits of Highly Effective People. Simon & Schuster, 1989.

NHS Mental Health. National Health Service England. https://www.england.nhs.uk/mental-health/

Robbins, Anthony. Awaken the Giant Within: How to Take Immediate Control of Your Mental, Emotional, Physical and Financial Destiny! Simon & Schuster, 1991.

"A hero is someone who has given their life to something bigger than themselves." – Joseph Campbell

CHAPTER 2

Your Hero's Journey: The Path to Reinvention

The journey from ordinary to extraordinary is the core of every captivating story. Joseph Campbell, a mythologist, created a framework called the Hero's Journey. It has impacted many stories, from old myths to new films like Star Wars, The Matrix, and Harry Potter. Even iconic Indian epics, including the Mahabharata and Ramayana, follow this structure. The Hero's Journey is a cyclical journey of transformation. It starts with a call to adventure. Then come trials and obstacles that shape the hero's growth. The hero comes back with new wisdom. They use their experiences to inspire and help others.

You might experience career stagnation, an uncertain future, or feel overwhelmed by change. Perhaps you're pursuing a goal, but you're tempted to quit. By understanding the Hero's Journey, you can plan the next steps. It chronicles transformation via challenges and growth. The Hero's Journey is not just a storytelling tool. It shows real-life growth, change, and breakthroughs. Each challenge you face and every obstacle you clear is a step in your journey of change. Most people do not act when there is a call for adventure because of various constraints. Some constraints include time, money, and relationships. They are explored in the later chapters. To navigate transformation, you first need to assess the current situation. Several techniques can help you assess where you are in life, each offering valuable insights.

One effective method is the Wheel of Life, a visual tool that evaluates different aspects of your life and helps to find imbalances. SWOT Analysis is another useful approach, allowing you to recognise your strengths, weaknesses, opportunities, and threats. Journaling and self-reflection give deeper insights through writing and introspection, while personality and behavioural assessments such as MBTI or Enneagram offer a better understanding of your traits and tendencies.

Seeking feedback can be valuable. A 360-degree feedback, where peers, mentors, or colleagues share their perspectives, can highlight strengths and blind spots. Goal-setting frameworks SMART Goals or Goal-Question-Context (GQC) offer structured ways to set and track progress. By using these tools, you can gain a clearer understanding of where you are, find areas for growth, and take meaningful steps toward transformation.

Self-assessment employs the Wheel of Life. It provides a holistic view of different aspects of life, helping you identify imbalances and set priorities for growth.

The tool depicts a circle divided into sections, each corresponding to different areas of life, such as career, finances, health, relationships, personal growth, recreation, and contribution. You rate your satisfaction in each category on a scale from one to ten, with one being unfulfilled and ten being satisfied.

Once plotted on the wheel, these ratings create a visual representation of a balance in your life. An uneven wheel highlights areas that may need more attention. For example, you might have a successful career but struggle with personal relationships or enjoy good health, but face financial instability. Recognising these imbalances allows you to take targeted action towards a more fulfilling and well-rounded life.

Using the Wheel of Life to Move Forward

To use the Wheel of Life, start by drawing your wheel and rating each category. find any imbalances and show on which areas need improvement. Pay attention to recurring patterns that may influence your overall well-being.

Once you gain clarity, set specific and realistic goals for growth. Tracking progress is essential—reassess your Wheel of Life to measure improvements and adjust your priorities as needed. This simple yet powerful tool keeps you focused on what matters. Success thus extends beyond a single domain, promoting a balanced, fulfilling existence.

Where are you on your Hero's Journey?

Start by reflecting on your life. What are the major challenges you have faced?. What stage of the Hero's Journey is in now?

Are you still in the ordinary world, feeling stuck? are you ready for the call to adventure? Or are you deep inside the Hero's journey facing challenges, searching for allies? Recognising your stage helps you prepare for what comes next.

Take the first step toward change if you're just starting out. If you're in the middle of challenges, seek mentors and allies. If you've had a breakthrough, focus on applying your growth in daily life. Every step forward brings you closer to becoming the hero of your own story.

You Are the Hero of Your Story

Your life follows the same transformational path as every glorious hero. Every challenge is a chance to grow. Every fear you conquer brings you closer to your true potential. Lewis Hamilton's journey to Formula 1 was a battle against odds. Raised in a working-class family in Stevenage, in England. His father worked multiple jobs—washing dishes and working in IT—just to fund his son's karting dream. Unlike wealthy rivals, Lewis had to make every opportunity count.

Balancing school with racing, he trained, knowing each race was a step closer to success. His breakthrough came in 1998 when McLaren and Mercedes recognised his talent. A decade later, he became the first Black F1 driver and, in 2008, the youngest world champion.

Facing a major obstacle strengthens your resolve. Life proceeds for most. You don't have to wait for some major painful experiences to awaken your full potential. Always remember that you have limited time. You can make this world a better place. A strong purpose inspires action and helps you explore your potential.

Time, money, and relationships can stop people from reaching their full potential. If you re-look at them, then you can craft a Life of Purpose and Fulfilment.

In the next chapter, you'll explore Finding Your True North. It focuses on purpose and meaning as the foundation for building a fulfilling future.

Questions for Reflection

- *What significant challenge or transition have you faced that felt like a turning point in your life? How did you respond to it?*

- *What aspect of your life currently feels the most out of balance? What does your Wheel of Life reveal about this?*

- *Was there ever a time you resisted calls to change or grow? What fears or doubts held you back?*

- *What resources, strengths, or allies might assist in your current journey?*

- *If your life were a Hero's Journey, what stage do you believe you are in right now? What step do you need to take next?*

References and Further Reading

Campbell, Joseph. The Hero with a Thousand Faces. Princeton University Press, 1949. A foundational work on the Hero's Journey, exploring the universal patterns of transformation found in myths and storytelling.

Vogler, Christopher. The Writer's Journey: Mythic Structure for Writers. Michael Wiese Productions, 2007. A modern adaptation of Campbell's Hero's Journey, widely used in storytelling, personal development, and leadership.

Covey, Stephen R. The 7 Habits of Highly Effective People. Free Press, 1989. A practical guide to self-improvement and proactive life design, closely related to tools like the Wheel of Life.

Robbins, Tony. Awaken the Giant Within: How to Take Immediate Control of Your Mental, Emotional, Physical and Financial Destiny! Free Press, 1991. Focuses on personal transformation, goal-setting, and taking action to reshape

"He who has a why to live can bear almost any how." – Friedrich Nietzsche.

CHAPTER 3

Purpose and Meaning: Finding Your True North

In 2018, Yvon Chouinard, the founder of Patagonia, made a radical decision. He said the company would donate $10 million saved from tax cuts to groups fighting climate change. It wasn't just a marketing move; it reflected Patagonia's deep-seated purpose—to protect the planet. Patagonia stands out from many corporations. Patagonia sees environmental responsibility as a key part of its business model. While others may view it as secondary, sustainability is a priority for Patagonia. Patagonia commits to using ethical materials and providing lifetime guarantees on its products. This approach isn't just about profit; it aims to create a lasting impact.

Patagonia's success shows the power of purpose. Many companies chase financial goals. Companies that have a clear mission beyond just making money connect better with employees and customers. Purpose drives people and organisations in business and life. It inspires them to keep going, innovate, and create a real impact on the world.

Purpose is the invisible force that shapes our actions, clarifies our decisions, and gives meaning to our existence. Without it, life can feel aimless. It may have fleeting pleasures and short-lived achievements, but it lacks true fulfilment.

In the UK, during the COVID-19 pandemic, Captain Tom Moore, a 99-year-old WWII veteran, set out to raise £1,000 for the NHS. He planned to walk 100 laps of his garden before his 100th birthday. His efforts touched hearts worldwide, raising over £32 million for NHS Charities Together. His determination and optimism symbolised hope. His words inspired many: "Tomorrow will be a good day." In July 2020, Queen Elizabeth II knighted him for his amazing fundraising efforts. Doctors hospitalised him with COVID-19 and pneumonia. He passed away on 2nd February 2021. Captain Sir Tom Moore's legacy lives on, proving that small acts of kindness can inspire the world.

Discovering the purpose is rarely straightforward. Others can't measure, quantify, or confirm it like they can with external achievements. It's very personal, always evolving, and often covered by conditioning, social expectations, and personal fears

Although complex, several methods can help uncover what truly drives an individual. In the next few sections various approaches are discussed very briefly but the important point is one needs to make an attempt to explore his/her purpose.

Ikigai is the Japanese philosophy of fulfillment. It is a Japanese idea that means "reason for being." It helps people find their purpose. By looking into these areas, people can find a purpose that is meaningful and lasting. The Ikigai framework helps you discover your purpose by finding the intersection of four elements: what you love, what you're good at, what the world needs, and what you can be paid for. When these areas align, they reveal a path that is both meaningful and sustainable.

The Reverse Bucket List is a perspective on regret-based thinking. Instead of asking what one hopes to achieve, it shifts the focus to what one would regret not doing. This shift in perspective can be eye-opening. It helps people find motivations that are often hidden by daily distractions.

Many people pursue goals that seem important in the moment, only to realise later that they lack real significance. Reflecting on life from the perspective of old age often brings clarity—it strips away societal expectations and reveals what truly matters. While it's possible to achieve almost any goal you deeply commit to, you can't achieve all goals. Every choice involves trade-offs; by choosing one path, you inevitably close the door on others. That's why being intentional about what truly matters is so important.

Mihaly Csikszentmihalyi's research shows that we find purpose in activities that deeply engage us and allow for effortless immersion. It is called the Flow state. When individuals enter a state of flow, they lose track of time, feel energised rather than drained, and perform at their best.

Recognising moments when work or activities feel effortless and fulfilling can provide valuable insight into an underlying passion worth pursuing.

The 5 Why's technique helps people dig into the real reasons for your choices. Our early motivations often come from conditioning or outside expectations. They tend to stay at a surface level. By asking why a goal matters, you can uncover the core values behind your goals.

For example, consider the person who says, "I want to make a lot of money." You can use the 5 Why's to explore further.

1. Why do you want to make a lot of money? - I can give a secure life to my family.

2. Why do you want to secure your family's life? - So that I can focus on starting my own business?

3. Why do you want to start your own business? – So that I can help society.

4. Why do you want to help society? Few people helped me with my education when I was growing up. I want to give back by building a school in my village.

5. Why do you want to build the school? – I love learning and teaching. Education has made a huge difference in my life and in the power of education to transform lives.

When a person understands that their purpose is about learning and education, they can begin to work towards it, also focusing on giving security to his family. Instead of building a school, he might start a YouTube channel to teach and take action..

Often, the best way to find purpose is not through introspection, but through action. Nike's famous slogan, "Just do it," captures this idea perfectly. Thinking too much can cause you to feel stuck. But taking steps towards your interests, even when unsure, gives you valuable feedback on what you really connect with.

Purpose doesn't always come before action. More often, it emerges through trial, error, and lived experience.

Non-finito in Italian means "unfinished". Michelangelo's unfinished sculptures remind us that not every endeavour needs to be completed to contribute to something meaningful. Embracing the freedom to start, explore, and let go without guilt allows purpose to evolve naturally over time.

The concept of non-finito offers the freedom to abandon pursuits that no longer resonate. Numerous individuals experience pressure to complete tasks, regardless of suitability.

Bangalore-based cognitive fitness coach Savitha SR was an IT professional. She became very interested in mind and memory techniques. At first, she thought she could be a teacher. After teaching for some time, she found her true passion in helping people with mid-life crises. Letting go of the paths that did not give her fulfilment helped her to find her niche.

The Misconception of "Start with Why"

Simon Sinek's famous TED Talk and book emphasised the importance of purpose, arguing that clarity around your why provides meaning and direction. However, purpose often becomes clear through experience rather than at the outset.

Many of the world's most successful individuals and organisations did not begin with a crystal-clear sense of purpose.

Instead, they evolved, experimented, and discovered their 'why' along the way.

The success stories we admire—like Apple's bold mission or Patagonia's purpose-driven brand—often feel like they were perfectly planned from day one. But the truth is, most of those philosophies were shaped over time, through trial and experience. Take Patagonia, for example. Yvon Chouinard didn't set out to build a global brand, and sustainability wasn't his starting point. He simply followed what he was passionate about and stayed true to his values. The impact came later—because he kept doing what felt right.

Finding your true calling is an iterative process. Purpose strengthens over time, but you don't need to wait for perfect clarity before taking action.

A Final Thought About Purpose

In today's world, purpose is often talked about so much that it risks becoming a cliché. The best way to discover it is to look beyond yourself—focus on serving others or contributing to something meaningful. If nothing inspires you right now, start small. Helping others, even in simple ways, often leads to a deeper sense of fulfilment and reveals a purpose you may not have expected.

You don't need absolute clarity about your purpose before you begin. Your first step can be as simple as starting the journey of discovering yourself. Exploring the profound question, "Who am I?". By treating this as your mission, you can explore different paths and opportunities without pressure.

In a world full of chances, distractions, and duties, purpose acts like a true north. It guides us along a path that matches our values, strengths, and dreams. It helps people get through tough times, change their lives, and live with purpose. This way, they don't just do what others expect. A purpose gives a meaning to your life. The meaning gives you a sense of fulfillment.

One can learn a great deal about life, purpose, and meaning from the following story.

In one of history's darkest times, Viktor Frankl, a neurologist and psychiatrist, found a truth that changed how we view human resilience. Imprisoned in Nazi concentration camps during the Second World War, he lost his home, his career, and his family. In a place where suffering felt endless, he saw something remarkable. Some prisoners, even while facing the same horrors, showed an unbreakable inner strength. They refused to surrender to despair.

What made them different? Frankl realised that survival was not just about physical endurance or luck. Those who persevered had something deeper—a sense of purpose. They clung to reasons to keep going: a loved one waiting for them, unfinished work, or a dream yet to be fulfilled. Even in suffering, they found meaning, while those who lost sight of a reason to live faded quickly.

Frankl himself carried a purpose. Before his capture, he had been working on a manuscript outlining his psychological theories. The Nazis destroyed it, but in his mind, he rewrote every word, determined to survive so he could share his insights with the world. Through his suffering, he developed what would become the foundation of his life's work—logotherapy, psychotherapy based on the idea that meaning is the driving force of human life.

One of his most profound realisations was this: while we cannot always control what happens to us, we can always control how we respond. Even in the worst of circumstances, we still possess the greatest freedom—the freedom to choose our attitude. In "Man's Search for Meaning", Frankl wrote:

> *"Everything can be taken from a man but one thing: the last of the human freedoms—to choose one's attitude in any given set of circumstances, to choose one's own way."*

This idea, born from unimaginable suffering, is what makes Frankl's work so powerful. It is not an abstract theory, but a truth forged in the hardest of conditions. His message is simple yet transformative: no matter where we are in life, we can find purpose.

Today, Frankl's lessons are more relevant than ever. We all face challenges like career setbacks, personal loss, and uncertainty about the future. His story reminds us that meaning isn't something we wait to find; it's something we create. A tough job can become fulfilling when we view it as a way to support our family. Personal loss can motivate us to help others in similar pain. Even suffering, when faced with courage, can make us stronger and wiser.

Frankl's work shows the power of purpose and meaning. It calls to anyone feeling lost or stuck. His life teaches us that the key question isn't, "What do I want?" but, "What does life expect from me?". We all have the power to answer that question—to rise, endure, and create meaning, no matter what life throws our way.

Goals, aspirations, plans are like a map and purpose is like a compass that shows you the right direction. Sense of direction gives clarity and fulfillment.

You might know your purpose but feel held back by time, money, or relationships. The next section explores these limitations and helps you find a more fulfilling life.

As Steve Jobs said in his Stanford commencement speech:

> *"The only way to do great work is to love what you do. If you haven't found it yet, keep looking. Don't settle."*

Questions for Reflection

- *What's your unfulfilled ambition?*

- *Think about Ikigai. Where do your passions, skills, social needs, and money-making chances meet?*

- *How can you use the Ikigai framework to refine your sense of purpose?*

- *If you were to create a 'reverse bucket list,' what are the things you would regret not pursuing in life?*

- *What steps can you take now to ensure you won't have those regrets?*

- *Viktor Frankl emphasised the power of choosing one's attitude in any circumstance.*

- *How do you see the challenges in your life? Could changing your perspective help you find more meaning in tough times?*

References and Further Reading

Ikigai, Hector Garcia and Francesc Miralles. Ikigai: The Japanese Secret to a Long and Happy Life. Hutchinson, 2017.

Frankl, Viktor E. (2006). Man's Search for Meaning. Beacon Press.

Chouinard, Yvon. (2005). Let My People Go Surfing: The Education of a Reluctant Businessman. Penguin Books.

Csikszentmihalyi, Mihaly. (1990). Flow: The Psychology of Optimal Experience. Harper Perennial.

Sinek, Simon. (2009). Start With Why: How Great Leaders Inspire Everyone to Take Action. Portfolio.

Brown, Brené. (2012). Daring Greatly: How the Courage to Be Vulnerable Transforms the Way We Live, Love, Parent, and Lead. Gotham Books.

PART II: CLEARING THE ROADBLOCKS

Undretsand and reframe the practical and emotional constraints that hold you back.

"Time stays long enough for those who use it."
– Leonardo da Vinci.

CHAPTER 4

Time—It Is About You

In today's fast-paced world, many people feel they don't have enough time. Busy schedules, long to-do lists, and constant duties can cause stress and fatigue. The real issue, however, isn't time. It's how individuals manage their energy, focus, and priorities. Time is one of the constraints that stops people from exploring their purpose.

A Zen master once said that what a person knows has little value unless they do something with it. This clear statement shows that how people think about time affects how they use it. Instead of attempting to control time, the key lies in managing oneself. The following story explores how a shift in mindset can transform the way time is perceived and utilised.

At a corporate offsite, a CEO and his leadership team gathered to address the growing concern of workload and productivity. The company invited time management experts, researchers, and consultants. They shared tips to boost efficiency. Among the speakers was a Zen master, who had reluctantly agreed to attend due to his long association with one of the company's directors.

On the first day of the offsite, after discussions on productivity methods, the Zen master shared his perspective. He talked about how simple Zen philosophy is. He suggested that everyone should sit in silence or meditate for fifteen minutes daily. The CEO responded with amusement, explaining that he barely had time to eat lunch due to his packed schedule. The Zen master smiled and advised that, in that case, he should sit for an hour each day. This paradoxical statement left the room in silence, prompting deep reflection. It suggested that the issue was not time itself but how people related to it. The busier a person claimed to be, the more they needed to slow down and reassess their approach.

People often equate time with the ticking of a clock, but the two are not the same. Time is a vast, continuous experience, while the clock is a human invention used to measure and segment it. The first pendulum clock, designed by Christiaan Huygens in 1656, was among the earliest attempts to regulate time. Before that, ancient civilisations used sundials to track the passage of the sun. Today, time is fragmented across different zones, reinforcing the idea that it is relative rather than absolute.

The experience of time varies depending on circumstances. Waiting for an important job interview can make a few minutes feel like hours, while a holiday with friends seems to pass in an instant. This variation shows that time is not merely about measurement but about how it is experienced.

As time can't be controlled, we should focus on managing ourselves well. There are two key principles that can help reshape this approach. The first is the understanding that it is impossible to complete everything. Regardless of how productive a person becomes, new tasks will always emerge, creating a never-ending cycle. Instead of attempting to finish everything, it is more beneficial to focus on what truly matters. The second principle is to embrace the first. Accepting that not everything can be done eases stress and helps you prioritise. When you internalise these principles, you stop chasing endless tasks. Instead, you start making thoughtful choices about how to use your time.

Rather than struggling with time, structured approaches can help manage workload more effectively. Capturing all tasks in one system prevents them from being scattered across multiple lists. This can be done using a notebook, an app, or a digital planner.

Tasks can be grouped into three categories:

- Quick tasks that take under five minutes

- Fixed events with a set time and date
- Flexible tasks that can be done anytime

Prioritisation techniques, such as the Eisenhower Matrix, can further refine this approach. Tasks that are both important and urgent should be handled immediately, while those that are important but not urgent should be scheduled. Tasks that are urgent but not important can often be delegated, and those that are neither urgent nor important should be eliminated.

One of the biggest challenges with time management is the illusion of urgency. Many tasks feel urgent due to external pressures, but not all urgency is real. Some managers or clients demand updates not because they are necessary but due to their anxieties. Frequent status updates and unnecessary check-ins can slow progress instead of making it more efficient.

Tools like Kanban boards and project trackers offer transparency without frequent interruptions. Separating urgency from importance helps regain mental clarity. This reduces stress and improves decision-making. Most people believe they need better time management skills, but in reality, they need a new way of thinking about time.

Rather than attempting to do more, they should focus on what truly matters. The CEO in the Zen master's story believed he had no time, yet he spent hours in inefficient meetings and unproductive routines. Many professionals feel overwhelmed not because they lack time but because they lack clarity on what is essential. Aligning actions with values and priorities helps create a meaningful and balanced relationship with time. Time is not something that can be controlled; it is an experience that can be shaped. Instead of trying to fit more into a schedule, a better approach is to redefine how work, focus, and productivity are approached.

Accepting that it is impossible to complete everything removes unnecessary pressure. Prioritising what adds value to life and work ensures that time is spent meaningfully. Reducing unnecessary urgency by focusing on high-impact activities creates space for deeper engagement. Developing habits that support clarity, focus, and well-being enhances overall efficiency and satisfaction. The key is not to have more time but to use the time that already exists in a way that aligns with personal and professional goals.

To summarise the key takeaways Time is not the clock—it is an experience shaped by perception and engagement.

You will never get everything done, so focus on what matters most. Urgency is often an illusion—differentiate between what is truly important and what is just noise. Use structured workload management techniques such as prioritisation, focus periods, and clear delegation. Adopt habits of mindfulness and reflection to improve how time is experienced. It is not about managing time—it is about managing yourself.

Using these principles can turn feelings of being overwhelmed into a sense of control. This way, time works for you instead of against you.

Activity: Reframing Time – A Self-Assessment and Action Plan

This exercise helps you rethink how you use your time. It shows you where to improve your focus and energy. You can then take steps to make your daily schedule more intentional and productive.

Step 1: assess your current time perception Take a moment to reflect on your daily and weekly schedule. Answer the following questions honestly:

When you think about time, what comes to mind first—the clock, deadlines, or experiences?

Do you often feel like you don't have enough time to complete important tasks?

What percentage of your day is spent on urgent but unimportant tasks versus high-value, meaningful work?

How frequently do you feel overwhelmed or rushed?

When was the last time you felt fully immersed and present in an activity without worrying about time?

How often do you plan your day intentionally versus reacting to external demands and interruptions?

Do you regularly engage in self-care, mindfulness, or reflective practices to manage your energy?

Write down your responses and take note of any recurring patterns.

Step 2: identify time drains and inefficiencies

Review your schedule from the past three to five days and track how you have spent your time. Make a list of: The top three activities that consumed most of your time.

Any moments where you felt distracted, unproductive, or overwhelmed. Times when you felt truly engaged and productive. From this, identify: Time drains – tasks, habits, or distractions that consume your time but add little value. High-value activities – tasks that contributed to meaningful progress and personal growth.

Step 3: apply the prioritisation matrix

Using the Eisenhower Matrix, categorise your activities into four groups: Important and urgent – tasks requiring immediate attention, such as deadlines and crises.

Important but not urgent tasks help with long-term goals. They don't need immediate action. Examples include skill development and strategic planning.

Urgent but not important – these tasks seem urgent but add little value. Examples include unnecessary meetings and constant emails.

Not urgent or important – these are activities that distract or waste time. Examples include too much social media and aimless browsing.

Shift tasks from less important areas to more valuable ones. You can do this by cutting, automating, or handing off work when you can.

Step 4: Create a time reallocation plan

Based on your findings, make three small but impactful changes to how you spend your time. Some examples include: Setting daily focus periods where you eliminate distractions and work deeply on important tasks. Implementing a 10-minute evening review to plan your next day with clear priorities. Reducing or delegating low-value tasks that consume unnecessary time. Scheduling at least one reflective or mindfulness practice each day to manage stress and gain clarity.

Step 5: commit to a 7-day experiment

For the next seven days, implement the changes you have identified. At the end of each day, write a short reflection on: What worked well? What was challenging? How did your perception of time shift? At the end of the week, evaluate your progress and adjust your approach as needed. Time is not something you control; it is an experience shaped by your focus, priorities, and mindset. Instead of feeling rushed or reactive, you can take ownership of how you engage with time. Practising intentional time management boosts your productivity. It also gives you more room for meaningful and fulfilling work.

Questions for Reflection

- *How do you see time—something to control or an experience to shape?*

- *What tasks or habits waste your time without adding value? How often do urgent but unimportant tasks take over your day?*

- *When was the last time you felt fully present and engaged?*

- *What small change could improve how you manage time and energy? If you had full control of your schedule, how would you spend your time?*

References and Further Reading

Allen, David. Getting Things Done: The Art of Stress-Free Productivity. Penguin, 2001. A foundational book on productivity and time management, offering a structured system for reducing stress and improving efficiency.

Christensen, Clayton M. How Will You Measure Your Life? Harper Business, 2012. Explores how business principles can be applied to personal fulfilment, focusing on purpose, relationships, and long-term impact.

Covey, Stephen R. The 7 Habits of Highly Effective People: Powerful Lessons in Personal Change. Free Press, 1989. A timeless guide to developing habits that foster leadership, responsibility, and effectiveness in both personal and professional life.

Clear, James. Atomic Habits: An Easy & Proven Way to Build Good Habits & Break Bad Ones. Avery, 2018. A practical approach to making small, consistent habit changes that lead to lasting improvements in time management and productivity.

Mithare, Raghavendra. Time Management. The Bystander, Available at: https://www.thebystander.org/time-management-2/ A contemporary perspective on effective time management strategies, focusing on prioritisation, energy management, and mindful productivity.

"Money is only a tool. It will take you wherever you wish, but it will not replace you as the driver."
– Ayn Rand

CHAPTER 5

Money: Its History, Psychology, and Mindset

Do you have enough money to lead a fulfilling life? If yes, what's stopping you from exploring your full potential? If no, do you know how much you truly need before you begin your journey?

It's not just the amount of money you have, but your relationship with it that shapes your quality of life and ability to embrace new opportunities.

While some people are very cautious even to spend a penny while on the other end some people are reckless and they keep spending on their credit cards and taking personal loans without even having the means to pay them off. Most wealthy people tend to be cautious; they also have the 'abundance' mindset rather than the 'scarcity' mindset.

Money has always shaped human civilization. It drives economies, affects individual lives, and influences global systems. Yet, many people misunderstand it. They chase it, fear it, or link it to security and success. Many people postpone living their dreams thinking they do not have enough financial backup. True financial well-being begins with understanding the origin of money. Understanding it's importance and limitations. It also requires recognising its psychological effects and developing the right mindset to build lasting wealth. More importantly having a peace of mind no matter how much you have in your bank.

The history of money began with the barter system, where people exchanged goods and services directly. While this allowed trade, it had its limits. For example, if someone had rice but needed shoes, the trade would only work if the shoemaker wanted rice in return. In order to solve the limitation of the barter system, societies developed commodity money, using valuable items like gold, silver, and salt as mediums of exchange.

The first metal coins appeared around 600 BCE in the ancient kingdom of Lydia, now modern-day Turkey. These coins were durable, portable, and standardised, making trade easier. Later, paper money emerged in China around the 7th century CE, offering a lighter, more practical alternative to metal coins.

As societies advanced, modern banking systems took shape, especially in Europe during the Renaissance. Institutions like the

Medici Bank introduced checks, promissory notes, and credit systems. By the 20th century, fiat money—currency not backed by physical commodities—became the global standard. This shift gave governments more control over the money supply.

Today, digital transactions and cryptocurrencies are reshaping financial systems, challenging traditional banking and driving the next evolution of money.

Money is simply a system of trust. Its value exists because people collectively believe it can be exchanged for goods and services of equal worth. Without this trust, money would be nothing more than paper, metal, or digital numbers with no real value.

Throughout history, money has not only influenced economies but also shaped human behaviour. It has strengthened thoughts on value, trade, and accumulation. This has changed how people see wealth and security.

People's relationship with money varies greatly. Some see it as a tool for freedom, others as a form of security, and some as a source of stress. Many beliefs about money stem from childhood experiences, cultural influences, and societal norms. Those raised in scarcity often believe money is hard to earn and must be saved carefully. Others view it as a resource for growth, investment, and new opportunities.

In his book Secrets of the Millionaire Mind, Harv Eker argues that a person's money blueprint largely shapes their financial success. This blueprint is made up of subconscious beliefs formed early in life. For example, someone who grows up hearing that money is the root of all evil or that wealthy people are greedy may unknowingly block their own financial growth.

In contrast, those who view money as a tool for opportunity and positive change tend to develop healthier financial habits. They are more likely to invest wisely, start businesses, and see wealth-building as an empowering journey rather than a struggle.

Society often links money with status, power, and success, fueling an obsession with accumulation. People are conditioned to believe that financial wealth is the ultimate measure of achievement.

Several psychological factors drive this mindset. Many compare their financial situation to others, creating pressure to maintain a particular image or lifestyle. Fear of not having enough also plays a role, as people worry about financial security even with ample resources. Additionally, the view of money as a tool for control strengthens its importance, giving individuals the freedom to make choices about their lives.

In his book The Psychology of Money, Morgan Housel says that money's real value isn't what it buys. Instead, it's about the freedom it brings. Many people forget that the real goal isn't just to build wealth. It's about having the freedom to make choices without financial stress. Many people chase money, thinking it will bring peace. But often, they feel more anxious and unhappy.

A common myth about money is that more wealth always brings more security. While financial stability matters, wealth alone doesn't guarantee peace of mind.

In "Rich Dad, Poor Dad," Robert Kiyosaki talks about how being rich is not the same as being wealthy. Many high-income earners still live paycheck to paycheck because they lack financial literacy. Many think security means earning more money. But real financial security comes from how you manage, invest, and grow your money over time.

Someone who earns a million dollars a year but spends it all is not financially secure. On the other hand, a person with a smaller income who regularly invests is building real financial stability. True financial freedom comes from making your money work for you through investments, passive income, and smart wealth-building strategies.

Your mindset about money plays a big role in financial success. In "Secrets of the Millionaire Mind," Harv Eker says wealthy people believe in abundance. In contrast, those who struggle often think about scarcity. Successful individuals take charge of their financial future instead of blaming their situation. They see chances where others see issues. They focus on growing their wealth instead of playing it safe.

Morgan Housel believes that managing money is more about behaviour than technical skills. Many think wealth comes from financial expertise, but true success with money relies on habits like patience, long-term planning, and emotional control. He also talks about the power of compounding, showing how small, steady financial decisions can lead to big growth over time. Real wealth isn't just about owning things—it's about having the freedom to make choices without financial stress.

In Rich Dad, Poor Dad, Robert Kiyosaki highlights the importance of financial education. Wealthy people focus on buying assets that generate income, while the poor and middle class often work just to earn money. Many aim for higher salaries instead of learning how to invest, which keeps them financially dependent. Understanding the difference between assets and liabilities is essential for breaking free from this cycle.

In Think and Grow Rich, Napoleon Hill focuses on the psychology of building wealth. He believes financial success starts in the mind, not with external factors. According to Hill, successful people have a clear vision, strong belief, and persistence in reaching their goals. Fear is a major obstacle, as many avoid risks or investments due to fear of failure. Those who build confidence and take smart, calculated risks are more likely to achieve financial success.

Understanding money isn't just about theory; it requires action. Building financial literacy is the first step toward creating wealth. Reading books on money management, investing, and business helps develop essential knowledge. Don't just focus on earning a salary. It's also important to acquire assets like real estate, stocks, or businesses. Practising delayed gratification helps you avoid impulse spending. This focus on long-term investments can lead to better financial stability.

Creating multiple streams of income reduces financial risk and boosts security. Relying on a single paycheck is risky, as job losses or unexpected expenses can cause financial stress. You can improve your financial health by exploring passive income options like rental properties or dividend investments.

Understanding the psychology of money is just as important as managing it. Many people develop emotional spending habits, making financial decisions based on impulses instead of logic. Taking a rational, goal-focused approach to money helps avoid unnecessary debt and encourages smarter financial choices.

Money is a vital part of life, but its true power lies in how it is used, managed, and invested—not just in how much is accumulated. History shows that while financial systems change, the core principles of wealth stay the same. Real financial security comes from understanding money, making smart investments, and building sustainable income streams instead of simply saving cash.

Society often equates wealth with success, but true financial well-being comes from controlling money instead of letting it control you. By changing your mindset, improving financial knowledge, and using proven wealth-building strategies, anyone can create lasting financial security and enjoy a life of freedom. Money isn't just about having more—it's about making it work effectively for you.

Activity: Re-evaluating Your Relationship with Money

This exercise helps you think about your money mindset. You will identify limiting beliefs and take steps to build a healthier, empowering relationship with your money.

Step 1: Reflect on Your Money Story

Take a few minutes to answer the following questions honestly:

What are your earliest memories of money? Did you grow up in an environment where money was abundant, scarce, or unpredictable?

What were you taught about money by your parents, teachers, or society? Were these lessons positive, negative, or neutral?

When you think about money today, what words or emotions come to mind? Do you associate it with stress, security, freedom, greed, or opportunity?

Do you believe that making money is easy or difficult? Why?

How do you feel when you spend money? Do you feel guilt, joy, or indifference?

How do you feel when you save or invest money? Do you feel empowered, worried, or unsure?

Write down your answers in a journal or a notebook. This will help you find any hidden beliefs that may affect your money choices.

Step 2: Identify Your Money Mindset Type

Which money mindset do you connect with the most based on your answers?

Scarcity Mindset: You think there's never enough money. You often feel anxious about finances, even when things are good.

Survival Mindset: You live from paycheck to paycheck. You only think about paying immediate bills and don't plan for the future.

Comfort Mindset: You have what you need to live well. But, you skip chances to build wealth due to fear or uncertainty.

Growth Mindset: You view money as a tool for freedom and chance. You look for ways to build wealth and achieve financial independence.

Understanding your mindset is the first step to reshaping it.

Step 3: Rewriting Your Money Beliefs

Pick a negative belief you have about money. Change it into a positive and empowering statement.

Examples:

Negative belief: "Making money is difficult, and I have to work hard to earn it."

"Money comes to me from many places as I create value and chances."

Negative belief: "Rich people are greedy and selfish."

Reframed belief: "Wealth helps me create a bigger positive impact on my family and community."

Negative belief: "I am not good at managing money."

Reframed belief: "I am learning and improving my financial skills every day."

Write down at least three reframed beliefs and repeat them to yourself daily.

Step 4: Take Action Towards Financial Growth

To build a stronger financial future, commit to one small action this week:

Read a book on financial literacy. Good options include *Rich Dad Poor Dad*, *The Psychology of Money*, or *Secrets of the Millionaire Mind.*

Start tracking your expenses for better financial awareness. Set up an automatic savings or investment plan, even if it is a small amount.

Create a financial goal for the next three months and outline steps to achieve it. Write down your chosen action and set a reminder to follow through.

Step 5: Reflect and Adjust

At the end of the week, take some time to review your experience:

Did you notice any changes in your thoughts or emotions about money?

What challenges did you face while trying to shift your mindset?

What is one habit or action you can continue to improve your relationship with money?

Building a healthy financial mindset takes time. By regularly re-evaluating your beliefs and taking small, consistent steps, you can create a positive and empowering relationship with money. This approach will help pave the way for long-term financial success.

Questions for reflection

- *What is the most important lesson you learned from this chapter about money and financial well-being?*

- *How has your mindset about money been shaped by your upbringing, experiences, or societal beliefs?*

- *What limiting beliefs do you have about money, and how can you reframe them into a positive mindset?*

- *What is the minimum amount of money if you had today, it would be sufficient for you to survive rest of the life?*

- *What is one small action you can take this week to improve your financial literacy or habits?*

- *How will you commit to using money as a tool for freedom and opportunity rather than stress or limitation?*

References and Further Reading

Eker, T. Harv. Secrets of the Millionaire Mind: Mastering the Inner Game of Wealth. HarperBusiness, 2005.

Housel, Morgan. The Psychology of Money: Timeless Lessons on Wealth, Greed, and Happiness. Harriman House, 2020.

Kiyosaki, Robert T. Rich Dad Poor Dad: What the Rich Teach Their Kids About Money That the Poor and Middle Class Do Not! Plata Publishing, 1997.

Hill, Napoleon. Think and Grow Rich. The Ralston Society, 1937.

Robbins, Tony. Money: Master the Game – 7 Simple Steps to Financial Freedom. Simon & Schuster, 2014.

Stanley, Thomas J., and William D. Danko. The Millionaire Next Door: The Surprising Secrets of America's Wealthy. Longstreet Press, 1996.

Kahneman, Daniel. Thinking, Fast and Slow. Farrar, Straus and Giroux, 2011.

Thaler, Richard H., and Cass R. Sunstein. Nudge: Improving Decisions About Health, Wealth, and Happiness. Penguin Books, 2009.

Dominguez, Joe, and Vicki Robin. Your Money or Your Life: Transforming Your Relationship with Money and Achieving Financial Independence. Penguin Books, 1992.

"The quality of your life is the quality of your relationships." – Tony Robbins

CHAPTER 6

Redesigning Relationships

A key part of your life that can hold you back is the quality of your relationships. These aren't just about the people around you. It also include how you relate to money, time, success—and most importantly, yourself. Every relationship affects your peace of mind, personal growth, and overall well-being. It is one of the constraint that stops you exploring your potential and design a life of fulfillment.

Your relationships—with your partner, parents, children, friends, boss, colleagues, and neighbours—impact your emotions and daily experiences. Often, the real issue in conflict isn't what someone does, but how you respond. Many conflicts follow repeated patterns you might not notice. In psychology, these are called "Rackets," a term from Transactional Analysis by Dr Eric Berne.

A racket is a behaviour pattern you keep repeating. Recognising these patterns can help you break free from conflict.

Rackets have 4 components. The first one is persistent complaints (he/she is again on the phone), then the next one is reaction to that complaint (feeling frustrated, angry). For example, if a colleague arrives late to meetings, you may react with frustration—maybe with a sarcastic comment or a loud sigh. This reaction makes you feel right and your colleague seems careless.

The next two elements are pay off and cost. In the above example the pay off for your racket is you get to be right and make the other person wrong. Human being have a very strong desire to be right. You continue the racket instead of resolving, it reinforces the belief that you're the only reliable one and others are not committed. While you continue the Racket since you do not pay attention to the underlying cost. The cost in any Racket is the loss of oneness, positive energy, joy and fulfillment.

When you notice this pattern along with the pay off and the cost, you can choose a different response—perhaps talking to your colleague directly or adjusting your expectations. This way, you free yourself from the frustration. Improve your work environment.

Rackets often revolve around ongoing complaints. Maybe your partner is always on their phone. Each time they check it, you react with irritation—making a comment or withdrawing. This keeps you feeling right and makes your partner seem wrong. Again, the cost is tension and distance.

You can overcome these rackets by letting go of the complaint as soon as you notice it. The need to be right often hinders closeness and connection. When you insist on being right, you create distance. The more you cling to your position, the less space you leave for empathy and growth.

Letting go of the need to be right doesn't mean ignoring issues—it means focusing on what truly matters: harmony and healthy communication. Instead of holding onto resentment, ask yourself, "Is this complaint worth losing closeness over?" Most of the time, it isn't. When you realise this, letting go becomes easier. When you stop blaming and start finding solutions, your relationships improve.

Understand that your ideas of right and wrong often come from social conditioning. Instead of behaving based on inherited expectations, create your own value system based on principles. For example, instead of respecting elders just because your culture says so, choose to respect all people. Then, respecting elders happens naturally—out of genuine belief. This shift takes you from "I have to" to "I want to."

Attachment in relationships is another dimensions to explore. It creates expectations—and unmet expectations lead to disappointment. Commitment, on the other hand, brings strength. It allows you to nurture relationships without needing perfection from others. Many struggles come from expecting others to meet emotional needs they may not know about. As Buddha said, "Expectations and desires are the root of all suffering." Letting go of attachment and embracing commitment eases emotional pain and helps you grow stronger.

Beyond people, you also have relationships with money and time—topics explored in the previous chapters. If money stresses you, you might believe it's hard to earn, tough to keep, and never enough. This mindset, called scarcity thinking, keeps you stuck in fear and hesitant to take risks. Others choose a different mindset. They see money as a tool for growth. They believe wealth comes from value, investment, and smart decisions. This is known as an abundance mindset.

Robert Kiyosaki, author of Rich Dad, Poor Dad, explained that wealthy people think differently about money. They don't just work for money—they make money work for them. Financial success isn't only about earnings. It's about how you think, manage, and invest. Your view of money shapes your financial reality.

Time is another vital relationship. Maybe you often feel there's never enough. You're overwhelmed by tasks and deadlines. But the issue isn't time—it's how you perceive and manage it. When you're focused, time feels spacious.

Zen philosophy teaches that slowing down can increase productivity. When you give your full attention to one task, you become more efficient and peaceful. There's a Zen saying: "If you don't have time to meditate for ten minutes, meditate for an hour." In other words, time isn't the problem—it's your attention and how you choose to use it.

There's a powerful modern take on a Buddhist story "The Two Arrows" shared by The Bystander Project, known as the "Three Bullets." It beautifully illustrates how much of your emotional suffering stems not from what happens to you—but from how you respond and what you imagine might happen next.

The first bullet is the pain life throws your way—things you cannot control. A breakup, a job loss, an argument, or a failure. This is the inevitable pain that everyone experiences. But then comes the second bullet—your reaction. This is where the suffering deepens: the rumination, the blame, the self-doubt. You replay what happened, judge yourself or others, and reinforce a story that keeps the pain alive. And then there's the third bullet—the one you fire at yourself in your imagination. It's the "What if?" or "If only…" loop. It's the fear of things that haven't even happened, or guilt over things you can't change. These imagined worries cause real stress and can damage your relationships, your peace of mind, and your sense of self-worth.

This teaching invites you to pause and ask: "Am I hurting from the first bullet, or am I adding the second and third myself?" When you learn to stop firing those second and third bullets, you reclaim your power. You begin to heal not just your relationships with others, but also your relationship with your own thoughts, emotions, and expectations. That's where true freedom begins. Pain is inevitable. Suffering is optional.

At the heart of every relationship is your mindset. It shapes how you experience life. It determines whether you see problems or possibilities, act with fear or confidence, and believe in growth or doubt. A fixed mindset says, "I can't change," leading to avoidance. A growth mindset says, "I can try, let me learn" opening the door to progress.

The most important relationship you have is with yourself. Every other relationship—with people, money, time, and success—reflects how you treat yourself. If you're harsh or unkind to yourself, you project that energy onto others. If you lack self-worth, you may accept poor treatment or block your success.

How you treat yourself determines how you treat everyone else. When you respect yourself, you set healthy boundaries. When you believe in your worth, you don't settle for less. When you care for yourself, you extend that care to others. Self-love isn't selfish—it's the foundation for all relationships. It's about accepting who you are while staying open to growth.

You don't see the world as it is—you see it as you are. If you shift how you relate to yourself, your entire experience transforms. When you treat yourself with kindness, you become more patient with others. When you believe in yourself, you attract better opportunities. Letting go of limiting beliefs opens the door to a richer life.

Every part of your life is shaped by relationships. Healing your relationships with others starts by letting go of expectations. Shifting your relationship with money means moving from fear to possibility. Improving your relationship with time starts with being present. Cultivating a growth mindset helps you face life with resilience. And nurturing a strong, compassionate relationship with yourself gives you the foundation for a meaningful life.

Marc Forster, Screenwriter & Director of "The Kite Runner" said this about letting go - "It was like I had been chasing after something and suddenly I just stopped and looked around me. I stopped inside and my mind became peaceful and clear. We don't know what it means to let go … to discover that nothing is permanent, and we invent numerous beliefs to protect us from the fear of letting go. We are frightened of letting go because we have postponed it. I believe that only through that act will my mind be free and able to experience what true freedom is."

When you master your relationships, you free yourself from fear, doubt, and scarcity. Life stops being a struggle and becomes something to enjoy.

Everything changes when you stop chasing happiness out there and start creating it within. And when you shift from "Me first" to "You first," you move from Me to We—transforming your mindset and your life.

In the next section you will explore designing a life around your purpose, setting and achieving meaningful goals.

Questions for reflection

What patterns do you notice in your recurring conflicts or complaints with others?

- *When similar situations happen, how do you usually respond?*

- *What might be the deeper story or belief behind this pattern?*

- *How has this pattern served you so far? And how has it limited you?*

What are you unconsciously expecting from others (or from yourself) that is creating disappointment, frustration, or suffering?

- *Are these expectations clear, fair, or even spoken aloud?*

- *How might your experience change if you shifted from expectation to acceptance or commitment?*

- *What would it feel like to relate to others and yourself without needing them to meet these hidden demands?*

Where in your life are you prioritising being "right" over being connected?

- *How important is it for you to be right in certain situations?*

- *What happens to your relationships when you hold onto being right?*

- *What might become possible if you focused on harmony and understanding instead?*

How are you treating yourself on a daily basis?

- *What is the usual tone of your inner voice?*

- *Are you kind, supportive, and respectful towards yourself, or more often harsh and critical?*

- *How might you begin treating yourself like someone you deeply care about?*

References and Further Reading

Berne, Eric. Games People Play: The Psychology of Human Relationships. Grove Press, 1964.

Berne, Eric. What Do You Say After You Say Hello? Corgi, 1975.

Covey, Stephen R. The 7 Habits of Highly Effective People: Powerful Lessons in Personal Change. Free Press, 1989.

Ruiz, Don Miguel. The Four Agreements: A Practical Guide to Personal Freedom. Amber-Allen Publishing, 1997.

Rosenberg, Marshall B. Nonviolent Communication: A Language of Life. PuddleDancer Press, 1999.

The Bystander Project. "The Three Bullets." The Bystander, https://www.thebystander.org/three-bullets/. Accessed 11 Feb. 2025.

PART III: DESIGNING A LIFE YOU LOVE

Craft a meaningful life by aligning your goals, enrgy and purpose

"The two most important days in your life are the day you are born, and the day you find out why." – Mark Twain.

CHAPTER 7

Designing a Life of Purpose and Meaning

"You have two lives, and the second begins when you realise you have only one." Mario de Andrade's poem 'My Soul is in a Hurry' captures the urgency to live fully. These words are a powerful reminder of the urgency to make the most of our precious time and realise our true potential.

This simple yet profound truth invites us to reflect on how we live. It calls us to move beyond hesitation and excuses, and instead, to embrace the present moment fully. But what does it really mean to live as if you have only one life?

This chapter invites you to pause and examine where you are today. When you accept that your first life — shaped by past choices and limitations — is already behind you, you create space for your second life to begin. Now is the time to build a new foundation. In later chapters, you will shape your goals and the path forward. You'll also encounter the principle of the Vector, which shows that life is not only about where you are heading, but also about the direction and energy with which you move.

Designing a life is an intentional and personal journey. It's not just about career—it's about crafting a meaningful life of purpose and clarity; it is about crafting a life that truly reflects who you are. Before setting professional goals or plotting your next move, it is essential to understand yourself — your strengths, passions, values, and dreams. This stage invites deep reflection, thoughtful questions, and meaningful choices. When you align these elements, professional success and personal fulfilment flow naturally.

The first step is to define your personal context. This is the lens through which you see yourself and the world. It helps you clarify your identity and identify what truly matters to you. Begin by reflecting on your current role, passions, values, and skills. Recognising that you are more than just a job title opens new possibilities. Your identity is a unique blend of experiences, talents, values, and aspirations. Understanding these elements gives you the power to make choices that feel authentic.

Start by reflecting on your current professional role and how you contribute to your field or community. Then, explore your passions — the activities that light you up, both in work and life. Passions often reveal what energises you and brings you joy.

Next, identify your core values — the principles that guide your choices and shape the way you interact with the world. Integrity, creativity, contribution, and freedom are examples of values that influence daily decisions, consciously or unconsciously.

Finally, reflect on your strongest skills, both technical and interpersonal. These are your natural gifts and cultivated talents, the abilities you enjoy using and that make a difference.

For example, someone might describe themselves as a leadership coach and personal branding expert who is passionate about helping people unlock their potential. Their values might include integrity, lifelong learning, and meaningful contribution. Their key skills could include strategic thinking, public speaking, and executive coaching.

To explore this for yourself, take a moment to write three to five sentences describing who you are. Go beyond your job title. Focus on your passions, values, and what makes you unique. What excites you? What gives you a sense of purpose?

A key part of life design is discovering what energises you. Work should not drain you — it should inspire you. Reflect on the moments when you feel most alive and deeply involved in what you are doing. When do you lose track of time? What types of problems do you enjoy solving? What topics do you naturally research, talk about, or create around?

Consider making two lists — five activities that bring you joy at work, and five that energise you outside of work. Then, look for patterns. Often, these lists reveal themes that can shape a more fulfilling career path.

Life design is not about fitting into old moulds — it is about making bold choices that match your strengths, passions, and values. This is how you create a life filled with purpose and possibility.

An essential question to ask along the way is: Who am I? Inspired by the Indian philosopher Sri Ramana Maharshi, self-inquiry helps you move beyond surface identities. Even a few minutes of this practice can bring unexpected clarity and calm.

When you repeatedly ask, Who am I?, you begin to strip away the labels. You are not just your body — you have one. You are not just your thoughts — you observe them. You are not defined by your job title, social roles, or achievements. Who are you beyond all of that? As you peel back these layers, you discover something deeper — pure awareness, simply I am.

Once you realise you are not limited by your roles or circumstances, you understand that you are free to choose who you wish to become. You are the creator of your life. You can consciously choose to see yourself as a leader, an artist, a change-maker — whatever feels true to you.

This is the foundation for creating a meaningful life: knowing yourself. When your work aligns with your deepest values and passions, it becomes a source of fulfilment, not just a means to earn a living.

Steve Jobs, in his famous 2005 Stanford commencement speech, shared how dropping out of college led him to a calligraphy course — seemingly a random choice. Yet, years later, that knowledge allowed him to design the first Macintosh with beautiful typography, which transformed digital design forever.

"You can't connect the dots looking forward," Jobs said, "you can only connect them looking backwards." His story is a reminder that unexpected choices often lead to profound discoveries.

Your vocation is more than your job title. It is the unique impact you make on the world. When you define your personal context, you begin to see clearly how your work, values, and aspirations align. Go beyond your current title and ask yourself:

- *What impact do I want to make?*

- *How do I contribute to my field or community?*

- *What excites me about my work?*

- *What values guide my decisions?*

For instance, instead of saying, "I am a leadership coach," you might say, "I am a catalyst for personal growth." This shift brings clarity and confidence, and it helps you see how you influence others.

Now, try this yourself. Write three to five sentences that describe who you are — not just your role — but what energises you, what you stand for, and the legacy you want to leave.

Designing a fulfilling life starts with knowing what brings you joy and energy. Reflect on when you've felt fully immersed in work. What challenges excite you? What topics do you explore passionately, even when no one is watching?

Your ideal work environment matters just as much. Do you prefer the structure of a corporate environment or the freedom of entrepreneurship? Do you enjoy collaborating in teams or working independently? Do you thrive in high-growth, fast-paced situations, or do you prefer the rhythm of steady and structured work?

Work should not only pay the bills but also enrich your life. Defining your personal goals helps you bridge today's actions with your long-term vision. What skills do you want to develop? What difference do you want to make? What legacy do you wish to leave?

Visualise your next three years. What work will you be doing? How will your skills grow? What impact will you have made?

Then, stretch further — imagine ten years from now. What legacy will you have built? How will you have influenced those around you? What will fulfilment look like for you?

Take one small action today — whether it's learning a new skill, reaching out to a mentor, or setting a clear intention — and begin shaping your future.

The Japanese concept of Ikigai — your "reason for being" — beautifully captures this balance. It lies at the intersection of what you love, what you are good at, what the world needs, and what you can be paid for. When these four elements align, you create a life that is meaningful, fulfilling, and sustainable.

Reflect on your Ikigai:

- Passion: Where what you love meets what you are good at.

- Mission: Where what you love meets what the world needs.

- Profession: Where what you are good at meets what you can be paid for.

- Vocation: Where what the world needs meets what you can be paid for.

Once you identify possible paths, take action. Test them through small experiments — a side project, a conversation with a mentor, or volunteering in an area of interest. Each step helps you refine your path.

Clarity and direction come from this process of self-discovery. As you align your work with your purpose, you may notice that the obstacles — time, money, or relationships — feel less overwhelming. The clearer your purpose, the smaller your constraints appear.

Questions for reflection

- *Who are you beyond your job title and social roles? What qualities, passions, and values truly define you?*

- *When have you felt most alive and fulfilled? What activities or situations made you lose track of time and feel fully engaged?*

- *What are your core values? Which principles guide your decisions and show you what really matters to you?*

- *What unique strengths and talents do you bring to the world? What abilities do you enjoy using most, and how do they make a difference to others?*

- *What impact do you want to create in your work, community, or relationships? What kind of legacy do you want to leave behind?*

- *What constraints are you currently facing — time, money, confidence, or relationships? How might these be shaping your choices? Could you view them differently?*

- *What does a meaningful and fulfilling life look like to you? How do you want to feel about your work and life three years from now?*

- *What patterns do you notice when you reflect on your passions and favourite activities? Are there recurring themes that could help you make better choices for your future?*

- *What is one small action you could take today to move closer to the life you want to design? How will this action help you align more closely with your purpose?*

References and Further Reading

- *Frankl, Viktor E. Man's Search for Meaning. Beacon Press, 1946.*

- *Csikszentmihalyi, Mihaly. Flow: The Psychology of Optimal Experience. Harper & Row, 1990.*

- *Sinek, Simon. Start With Why: How Great Leaders Inspire Everyone to Take Action. Portfolio, 2009.*

- *Dweck, Carol S. Mindset: The New Psychology of Success. Ballantine Books, 2006.*

- *Zaffron, Steve, and Dave Logan. The Three Laws of Performance: Rewriting the Future of Your Organization and Your Life. Jossey-Bass, 2009.*

- *Mithare, Raghavendra. "Vector: Where Do You Want to Go Today?" LinkedIn Articles, May 26, 2022. https://www.linkedin.com/pulse/vector-where-do-you-want-go-today-raghavendra-raghav-mithare/*

- *Mithare, Raghavendra. "Exploring Happiness" LinkedIn Articles, April 8, 2016. https://www.linkedin.com/pulse/exploring-happiness-raghavendra-raghav-mithare/*

"If you want to be happy, set a goal that commands your thoughts, liberates your energy, and inspires your hopes." – Andrew Carnegie.

CHAPTER 8

The GQC Framework: Rethinking Goals

Goals are more than just wishes or fleeting thoughts. They are milestones. They shape our actions, guide our paths, and bring satisfaction when reached. Without clear goals, we react to life rather than create it. Think of a sailor setting off without a destination. At first, drifting may feel exciting. But without a clear direction, the sailor will soon feel lost.

Life without goals is similar. Lacking direction makes it easy to procrastinate, feel uncertain, and miss out on fulfilment.

Ray Dalio, a successful investor and author of Principles, compares life to a machine where inputs lead to outputs. He warns that without clear goals, people move aimlessly and can't measure their progress. Dalio suggests that individuals should define what they truly want, figure out how to achieve it, and create a plan. The clearer the goal, the easier it is to face challenges and stay focused.

Steve Jobs, co-founder of Apple, understood the value of clear goals. When he returned to Apple in 1997, the company had a cluttered product line and no clear path.

Jobs made a bold move—he cut Apple's offerings to just four products, ensuring each was the best in its category. This focus turned Apple into a hugely successful brand.

Setting a goal is just the first step. The real challenge lies in choosing the right goals—those that match our values, sustain motivation, and keep us engaged through obstacles.

Many struggle to reach their goals. The three main reasons for this are lack of clarity, misalignment with personal values, and fear of failure.

A goal without clarity is just a wish. Many set vague goals like "I want to be healthier" or "I want to be successful," but without a clear plan, progress is hard to track.

Jack Ma, founder of Alibaba, believed success requires a clear vision. His goal was more than e-commerce; he aimed to build a digital ecosystem for small businesses worldwide. This vision kept him motivated through years of challenges.

Tony Robbins, a well-known motivational speaker, insists that goals must be specific, measurable, and time-bound. Instead of saying, "I want to be fit," a better goal would be, "I will lose 5kg in two months by exercising four times a week and following a structured diet."

This detail offers clarity, sets a measurable target, and defines a timeframe—making the goal much easier to achieve.

Another reason people fail to meet their goals is misalignment with personal values. Many set goals based on what society expects instead of what they truly want.

A young professional might study law to make their family happy, even if they really love creative writing. Someone might chase a well-paid job but feel empty inside. It may not match their true values.

Ray Dalio stresses that authenticity is key in goal-setting. To find meaningful goals, ask yourself why you want them. Will achieving them bring lasting joy? Do they align with your strengths and passions?

When goals are clear and authentic, they inspire rather than stress.

Fear of failure is a major barrier to success. The fear of stepping outside our comfort zone creates an invisible wall between where we are and where we want to be.

However, failure isn't the opposite of success; it's part of the journey. Dalio describes this as "pain plus reflection equals progress." The most successful people don't fear failure; they use it as a growth tool.

In 1938, Károly Takács, Hungary's best shooter, was ready for Olympic glory until an accident destroyed his right hand, crushing his dreams. For many, this would be the end. For Takács, it was just the beginning.

Determined to succeed, he trained to shoot with his left hand. A year later, at the Hungarian national championship, others thought he was there to support the team, but he said:

"I didn't come to watch. I came to compete."

He not only competed—he won.

When World War II delayed the Olympics, he waited and trained. Finally, in 1948, a decade after his accident, he won Olympic gold, setting a world record. In 1952, he did it again.

Takács showed that setbacks don't define us—our reactions to them do. His story is a powerful reminder:

The only real failure is giving up.

Many know about SMART goals—Specific, Measurable, Achievable, Realistic, and Time-bound. While this method offers structure, it often misses the deeper reason behind the goal. The Goal-Question-Context (GQC) framework refines SMART goals, ensuring they are clear, actionable, meaningful, and sustainable, aligning with a bigger purpose.

The GQC Framework offers a structured way to set and achieve meaningful goals through three steps. First, define a clear, measurable goal. Vague aims like "I want to be successful" or "I want to be happier" make tracking progress tough. Instead, a specific goal like "I will complete a leadership certification in six months" gives clear direction and measurable results.

The second step is to ask the right questions. Many set ambitious goals but forget to evaluate what they need to achieve them. Questions like "What skills must I develop?" or "Who can mentor me?" help clarify the goal and foresee challenges.

The third and most crucial step is establishing the context—the deeper reason behind the goal. This step builds emotional resilience, helping you push through setbacks. When motivation fades, the "why" behind a goal anchors you, keeping you moving forward.

If motivation is only external, like "It will look good on my LinkedIn profile," success is less likely due to weaker commitment. However, when motivation is intrinsic and aligned with your purpose—like "I want to create more leaders"—the goal gains deeper meaning, increasing the chance of success.

Thus, the goal "I want to complete a leadership certification in six months," becomes "To create more leaders and empower them, I will complete the leadership certification in six months." This showcases the power of the GQC Framework—it helps set goals that are meaningful, achievable, and aligned with your values.

Now, take a moment to reflect on what you truly want to achieve. Consider these questions to shape and refine your goals:

What is one goal you want to achieve in the next six months? Why is this goal important to you? How will achieving this goal improve your life? What specific steps will you take to move towards this goal? What challenges might you face, and how will you overcome them? What resources or support do you need? How will you measure your progress? What will keep you motivated when things get tough?

Make a habit of writing down your answers and reviewing them often. Gaining clarity, asking the right questions, and anchoring your goal in meaning can greatly boost your chances of success.

Understanding goals helps you set meaningful ones. While you can achieve goals with focus and dedication, you can't achieve all of them. You must choose which ones to commit to and which ones to let go. For instance, you can't aim to "enjoy life" by being lazy, sleeping in, and binge-watching TV while also being fit and working on your side hustle. You can't choose to stay in a familiar place and explore the world at the same time. Weigh the trade-offs before setting your goals.

Every action has primary and secondary consequences. Eating a big slice of chocolate cake every night brings immediate pleasure (first-order), but later it leads to weight gain and poor health (second-order). In contrast, going to the gym may feel tough at first (first-order), but over time, it results in better health and confidence (second-order). Wise decisions consider both immediate effects and long-term outcomes.

Avoid chasing too many goals at once. Jack Ma shared a story about catching chickens to show the power of focus. He said if you try to catch all the chickens at once, you'll end up with none. But if you focus on catching one chicken patiently, you will succeed. In life and business, people often chase too many things and achieve little. The key is to focus on one clear goal and commit fully to it.

In the Bhagavad Gita, a key teaching about action and results is captured in this famous verse:

"Karmanye vadhikaraste, ma phaleshu kadachana" (Bhagavad Gita 2.47)

It means: "You have the right to perform your actions, but you are not entitled to the fruits of your actions."

The Gita teaches that you should focus on doing your actions (duty) sincerely, without attachment to the results. Outcomes are influenced by many factors beyond your control. When you act without being tied to success or failure, you find peace and wisdom. This principle encourages detachment from results and living in the present moment. Focusing on the action.

Daniel Kahneman, Nobel Prize-winning psychologist, stressed that success is not just about talent and effort, but also a great deal of luck. He warned against the illusion of control — the false belief that we control more than we do. People often credit success to skill or strategy alone, but Kahneman reminded us that chance plays a much bigger role than we like to admit, and humility is essential when judging success.

The path to success is never a straight line. It is filled with challenges, obstacles, and failures. Fear only tests your courage, not your limits. People who face their fears and take action, even when unsure, are the ones who achieve greatness.

Will failure occur? Absolutely—it is inevitable. But will you let it define you? Or will you rise, learn from it, and keep moving forward?

Yes, you will move forward.

In the end, context is decisive. It is the why behind everything you do. Life isn't always about changing circumstances, but changing how you see them. A shift in context unlocks new possibilities, makes the impossible doable, and turns burdens into opportunities. Don't just seek answers — shift the context, and everything changes.

Questions for Reflection

- *What Goals are you pursuing now? If you were to look back five years from now, would you regret not pursuing this goal?*

- *Are you setting this goal for yourself or trying to meet someone else's expectations?*

- *What deeper purpose or vision will keep you moving forward when motivation fades?*

- *What will you have learned if you fail that makes the journey worthwhile?*

- *If you had to achieve this goal in half the time, what would you prioritise or change?*

References and Further Reading

Dalio, Ray. (2017). Principles: Life and Work. Simon & Schuster.

Robbins, Tony. (1991). Awaken the Giant Within: How to Take Immediate Control of Your Mental, Emotional, Physical and Financial Destiny! Free Press.

Sinek, Simon. (2009). Start with Why: How Great Leaders Inspire Everyone to Take Action. Portfolio.

Swami Swarupananda. (2015). The Bhagavad Gita. Ramakrishna Math.

Iyer, P.rakash (2011). The Habit of Winning. Penguin Books India.

Covey, S. R. (1989). The 7 Habits of Highly Effective People. Free Press.

Clear, J. (2018). Atomic Habits: An Easy & Proven Way to Build Good Habits & Break Bad Ones. Avery.

Mithare, R. (2023). GQC: Goal-Question-Context – Don't Start with Why. The Bystander. Available at: https://www.thebystander.org/dont-start-with-why/

Kahneman, Daniel. (2011). Thinking, Fast and Slow. Farrar, Straus and Giroux.

"Efforts and courage are not enough without purpose and direction." – John F. Kennedy.

CHAPTER 9

Vector Thinking: Aligning Speed & Direction

The journey from ordinary to extraordinary is the core of every captivating story. Joseph Campbell, a mythologist, created a framework called the Hero's Journey. It has impacted many stories, from old myths to new films like Star Wars, The Matrix, and Harry Potter. Even iconic Indian epics, including the Mahabharata and Ramayana, follow this structure. The Hero's Journey is a cyclical journey of transformation. It starts with a call to adventure. Then come trials and obstacles that shape the hero's growth. The hero comes back with new wisdom. They use their experiences to inspire and help others.

In physics, a vector is defined as an entity possessing both direction and magnitude. This scientific principle serves as a powerful metaphor for life—illustrating why some individuals navigate their path with purpose and achievement while others struggle to find direction despite their persistent efforts.

Too often, individuals find themselves in one of two situations. Some are highly ambitious, relentlessly chasing goals, yet they often experience a sense of emptiness, as if their achievements feel hollow. Others embrace life as a journey, going with the flow, but they struggle with stagnation, feeling as if they are drifting without truly achieving anything meaningful.

The concept of a vector helps resolve this paradox. To create a fulfilling life, one must have both direction: a clear sense of purpose, and magnitude: the energy and pace of action.

This idea is not merely theoretical; it is evident in the lives of history's most successful and influential figures. Whether in business, science, or the arts, those who leave a lasting impact share a common trait: they move with both purpose and momentum.

Direction in life means having a well-defined purpose. Without it, even the fastest progress becomes meaningless. It is like the Japanese saying: "If you get on the wrong train, get off at the next station; the longer you stay on, the more expensive the return trip will be.'

A person can work tirelessly towards a goal, but if they are moving in the wrong direction, their efforts will fail to bring lasting fulfilment.

Steve Jobs, the visionary co-founder of Apple, exemplifies this principle perfectly. In his early years, Jobs was renowned for his intense drive and unwavering commitment to innovation. After being ousted from Apple in 1985, he faced a period of uncertainty. This was widely viewed as a career-ending setback, but Jobs used the time to refine his direction. He founded NeXT and Pixar, honing his skills in technology and design while expanding his creative vision.

When he returned to Apple in 1997, he brought a renewed sense of purpose that enabled him to transform Apple into a global powerhouse. Jobs' story illustrates that direction is not just about moving forward but about aligning actions with a meaningful destination.

If direction is about knowing where to go, magnitude determines the intensity and speed of action. Magnitude is the force that turns dreams into reality. Even with a clear vision of their goals, without action, that vision never materialises.

Ritesh Agarwal the founder of OYO Rooms, exemplifies the power of magnitude in action. At just 19, he envisioned revolutionising budget hospitality in India. However, having an idea was not enough—he needed to act swiftly, take risks, and relentlessly execute his vision. With sheer determination, he scaled OYO from a single-budget hotel into a global hospitality chain. His rapid execution, bold decision-making, and ability to attract investment transformed the industry.

His success was not built on talent and ideas alone. It was his unyielding discipline, persistence, and unwavering pursuit of his goal that propelled him to success. His magnitude—his speed and intensity—was what turned his vision into reality.

Magnitude thrives on discipline, consistency, and resilience. It sustains perseverance despite challenges and distinguishes fleeting ideas from world-changing achievements.

Ratan Tata's journey exemplifies the power of balancing direction with magnitude. His ethical leadership and bold ventures transformed the Tata Group into a global powerhouse. His vision has always been clear—businesses should strive for more than profit, contributing to a greater good. However, what truly sets him apart is his drive—the decisive speed and intensity with which he brings his ideas to life.

When Tata Motors launched the Tata Nano, the world's cheapest car, the goal was to make mobility affordable for millions in India. Despite challenges, Tata remained committed to his vision. Instead of abandoning the project, he recalibrated his approach, optimising both production efficiency and distribution networks.

His determination—his ability to take action, experiment, and adapt—kept Tata at the forefront of innovation while ensuring his mission remained intact. His journey exemplifies how a clear vision, combined with relentless execution, drives lasting impact.

Some individuals focus solely on magnitude—working tirelessly, pursuing goals, and striving for success—yet without clear direction. This cycle often leads to burnout, frustration, and a lingering sense of emptiness.

Many professionals and entrepreneurs face this challenge. They spend years climbing the corporate ladder or building businesses, only to realise too late that they never truly defined their purpose. Without a meaningful objective, even the most remarkable achievements can feel hollow.

On the other hand, some individuals have a strong sense of purpose but lack the magnitude—the speed and drive—to act upon it. They may possess a clear vision and noble intentions, but without action, their dreams remain unfulfilled.

A classic example is Nikola Tesla, a visionary whose ideas often surpassed the technological possibilities of his era. His contributions to electrical engineering were groundbreaking. However, he struggled to commercialise many of his inventions. His limited business acumen and execution skills meant that many of his groundbreaking ideas remained underfunded or were overshadowed by competitors.

Though his impact on the world was immense, his story underscores the vital role of execution in bringing vision to life.

Ultimately, true success requires cultivating both direction—a clear sense of purpose—and magnitude, the speed and drive needed to turn ambition into reality.

The journey begins with clarifying your purpose and defining a clear direction. It starts by asking, "Where do I want to go? Why do I want to go there?" The purpose is deeply personal and evolves over time, but having a guiding direction ensures that every effort carries meaning.

The next step is assessing magnitude. It is essential to ask, "How fast and intensely should I move toward my goal?" At times, steady progress is necessary; at others, decisive and assertive action is required. Knowing when to accelerate is crucial. Equally important is recognising when to pause and reflect.

The final step is continual reassessment and adjustment. Life is rarely straightforward, as challenges, shifting priorities, and evolving perspectives shape our journey. Consistent reflection helps maintain alignment with one's true path.

History's greatest successes stem from individuals who mastered the balance between direction and magnitude. Whether it was Steve Jobs refining his purpose, Ritesh Agarwal moving with intensity, or Ratan Tata executing his vision with resilience, each embodied this vital principle.

The key lesson is that while having a clear direction is important, the velocity at which one moves forward is equally crucial. Speed matters, but one should not be reckless. As John Wooden, the legendary basketball coach at UCLA, used to say, "Don't rush but be quick."

Applying the vector concept to life offers a structured approach to achieving success and fulfilment. Whether in career, relationships, personal growth, or creativity, clear direction and consistent action lead to lasting impact and happiness.

The real question remains: Where are you headed, and how quickly do you want to arrive?

Now is the time to reflect, decide, and take action.

Questions for Reflection

- *Am I clear about my purpose and direction?*

- *Am I moving toward my true purpose or following external expectations?*

- *Am I acting consistently and with enough speed to achieve my goals?*

- *Have I ever moved quickly in the wrong direction? What did I learn?*

- *What's slowing me down, and how can I overcome it?*

- *Do I regularly refine my direction to stay aligned with my purpose?*

References and Further Reading

Mithare, Raghavendra. Vector: Success – Direction and Magnitude in Life. Available at: https://www.thebystander.org/vector/

Sinek, Simon. Start with Why: How Great Leaders Inspire Everyone to Take Action. Portfolio, 2009. An exploration of purpose-driven leadership and decision-making.

Wooden, John. Wooden: A Lifetime of Observations and Reflections On and Off the Court. McGraw Hill, 1997.

Robbins, Tony. Unshakeable: Your Financial Freedom Playbook. Simon & Schuster, 2017.

Robbins, Tony. Tony Robbins Interview with Coach John Wooden. https://tonyrobbins.libsyn.com/-the-legendary-john-wooden-an-interview-with-tony-robbins-what-it-means-to-build-character-be-a-true-leader-and-win-the-game-of-life?

PART IV: KEEPING THE MOMENTUM

Stay motivated, navigate uncertainty, and practice resilience with clarity

"The real problem is not whether machines think but whether men do." — B. F. Skinner.

CHAPTER 10

Navigating Uncertainty: AI and You

A key element of future planning is anticipating the impact of Artificial Intelligence (AI) transformations. AI plays a vital role in shaping our tomorrows. It is transforming industries, careers, and how we live, learn, and connect.

Entrepreneurs, professionals, and students alike need to understand AI's impact. Rather than fearing AI, learn to use it to your advantage. Effective use can boost our capabilities and unlock potential.

Picture yourself waking up to an AI assistant. It plans your day, recommends breakfast ideas, and composes your emails before you've finished your coffee. Artificial intelligence is transforming our daily lives, affecting how we work, think, and communicate.

AI's journey began in 1956. At the Dartmouth Conference, researchers sought to build artificially intelligent machines.

The computing power of the 1980s restricted the potential of early AI systems like expert systems, despite their promise. Following this, there were AI winters—times of slow progress and disappointment. Big data, machine learning, and deep learning drove significant advancements in AI during the 2010s.

The year 2012 marked a turning point with AlexNet's success in image recognition using deep learning. This resulted in swift advancements. AlphaGo's 2016 victory over a Go world champion was a breakthrough, previously considered impossible for AI. Advancements in GPUs (Graphics Processing Unit) enabled this growth. The 2020s saw models such as GPT-3, ChatGPT, and AlphaFold transform creative writing, drug discovery, and other fields.

AI, however, involves risks. Experts caution that uncontrolled growth might result in serious difficulties. Yuval Noah Harari, a historian and futurist, expresses concern that AI may undermine democracy. Such a thing may shift actions, causing digital autocracies. AI algorithms can manipulate human psychology to spread misinformation, influencing political discourse and creating personalized propaganda.

Society can benefit from AI, provided people stay watchful. The key question is not just what AI can do; it's how we ensure it helps rather than controls us.

The unique strength of Human intelligence is creativity, the ability to imagine. Jack Ma and Yuval Noah Harari highlight the vital differences between human and artificial intelligence. Their insights remind us what makes us irreplaceable. While AI revolutionises industries and automates tasks, it cannot replicate core aspects of human nature. Jack Ma, co-founder of Alibaba, believes AI can manage vast data and enhance efficiency. However, he argues it lacks true human creativity. Machines can create art, music, and stories by recognising patterns, but they cannot dream, imagine, or feel.

AI cannot innovate like humans. It lacks the deep emotions that inspire great art, literature, and entrepreneurship. Ma believes the future belongs to those who value creativity, think independently, collaborate, and care for others. These traits define human excellence beyond just technical skills. He often says education should focus on more than just tech. It should also nurture emotional intelligence, critical thinking, and strong interpersonal skills.

Yuval Noah Harari warns that while AI can excel in some tasks, it lacks consciousness and true understanding. A machine can diagnose diseases, craft convincing arguments, or mimic emotions, but it does not grasp its actions. AI cannot feel love, joy, or sorrow. It cannot ponder its existence or seek meaning. Harari asserts that while AI can make data-driven decisions, it lacks human wisdom, ethics, and the ability to navigate moral dilemmas.

The main message is clear: while AI may change the world, it is human intelligence, creativity, and compassion that will shape the future. Machines can carry out commands but do not experience true feelings. They can simulate emotions but do not genuinely feel. In Toy Story, we may be moved by the characters' emotions, yet they are just animated figures without real feelings. AI can generate solutions but lacks understanding of their deeper purpose. The challenge is not whether AI will surpass humans, but how we use this technology to enhance our potential, not replace it. In a world driven by AI, our unique qualities of imagination, wisdom, and empathy will guide us.

As AI evolves, you must take steps to navigate changes wisely. Instead of fearing automation, view AI as a tool. Focus on your unique human strengths. By adopting the right mindset, developing new skills, and embracing change, you can thrive in an AI-driven world.

The rise of AI requires a shift in your career approach. One key step is to stay adaptable. AI is advancing quickly, and many jobs will change significantly in a few years. Relying only on routine tasks could leave you behind. Commit to lifelong learning and stay curious about new technologies. Keeping up with industry trends and acquiring new skills will keep you relevant. Studying the impact of AI in your industry should be part of your planning.

Creative and critical thinking are crucial skills to develop. While strong logical reasoning is valuable, broader thinking is essential, especially in our AI-focused age. AI is powerful but not always accurate or ethical. Question AI decisions, recognise the limits of automation, and use technology responsibly. If you're in a leadership role, promote ethical AI practices to ensure it benefits people and preserves human agency.

To not just survive but thrive in an AI-driven world, focus on areas where human abilities far exceed those of machines. Creativity and innovation are among the most vital skills. AI can generate content and analyse patterns, but it cannot truly imagine or create with originality. Whether you work in business, design, science, or the arts, thinking outside the box is key. Fresh ideas and creativity will make you stand out.

Emotional intelligence and interpersonal skills are also vital. Though AI can mimic emotions, it does not understand human relationships deeply. Your ability to lead, empathise, and build trust is irreplaceable. If you can inspire others, mentor teams, and foster cooperation, you will remain essential, no matter how technology advances.

Developing strategic thinking and problem-solving skills will ensure long-term success. While AI can process data and suggest solutions, it cannot make complex, context-driven decisions. Your ability to see the bigger picture, anticipate challenges, and make informed ethical choices will position you for leadership roles and meaningful change.

The Future Belongs to Those Who Adapt. Instead of fearing AI, embrace it as an opportunity to advance your career and unlock your potential. Stay adaptable, develop uniquely human skills, and view AI as an enabler, not a threat. The goal is not to compete with machines, but to master the qualities that make you uniquely human. In this new era, those who embrace change, lead with vision, and use technology wisely will thrive and shape the future.

The choice is yours—step forward with confidence and let AI work for you.

Questions for reflection

- *Do you see AI as a threat or a tool for growth?*

- *What human strengths do you have that AI can't replace?*

- *How can you adapt and stay relevant in an AI-driven world?*

- *How will you use AI ethically and responsibly?*

- *How can you leverage AI to innovate rather than fear it?*

- *What action will you take today to ensure AI serves humanity?*

References and Further Reading

Harari, Yuval Noah. 21 Lessons for the 21st Century. Jonathan Cape, 2018. An exploration of how AI is shaping society, politics, and the future of human intelligence.

Kurzweil, Ray. The Singularity Is Near: When Humans Transcend Biology. Viking, 2005. A visionary perspective on AI's exponential growth and its implications for humanity.

Russell, Stuart, and Norvig, Peter. Artificial Intelligence: A Modern Approach. Pearson, 2020. A foundational textbook covering AI's history, applications, and future directions.

Bostrom, Nick. Superintelligence: Paths, Dangers, Strategies. Oxford University Press, 2014. A critical examination of the risks of AI surpassing human control.

Musk, Elon. Public statements on AI safety and risks. Highlights concerns about AI surpassing human control and the need for regulation.

Ng, Andrew. AI for Everyone (Coursera Course). A beginner-friendly introduction to AI's role in business, technology, and society.

OpenAI Research Papers and Blogs. Covers advancements in AI models, ethical considerations, and future developments in artificial intelligence.

"Success is not the key to happiness. Happiness is the key to success. If you love what you are doing, you will be successful." – Albert Schweitzer

CHAPTER 11

Happiness: The True Measure of Success

Happiness is something you seek by nature. No matter where you come from, what you do, or how old you are, you want to be happy. People define happiness in many ways. You know those moments when you feel a deep sense of happiness. After you meet your basic needs, you may start looking for more. You seek a lasting happiness that success or possessions cannot provide completely. You may have thought that you will be happy once you are successful. But what if it is the other way around? What if you will be successful because you are happy?

The good news is, you do not have to keep guessing. You can understand and even design your own happiness. As you begin to explore it more closely, you will discover that happiness is not just one feeling — it has three powerful dimensions. These dimensions are pleasure, engagement, and meaning. Each of them has something valuable to offer, and when you combine them, you find a deeper and longer-lasting happiness.

Pleasure is the happiness you get from simple, enjoyable activities — the little sparks of joy that often appear without much effort. You might feel happy when you sit down to watch a football match, whether it's your favourite team or just a casual game. You may enjoy listening to a beloved song, letting the music lift your mood or bring back a beautiful memory. Or you might delight in eating your favourite dish, savouring each bite and taking comfort in the familiar taste it brings. These small pleasures matter. They lift your spirits and add colour to your daily life.

Yet, if you rely solely on pleasure, you may begin to notice that its effects don't last. You might catch yourself thinking, "I want more," only to find that repeating the same activity doesn't bring the same joy as before. The happiness begins to fade. The first ice cream may make you smile, but the second won't double the happiness — it may even dull it. By the fifth, you might start to feel uncomfortable or even regretful. Over time, these pleasures can become mechanical, losing their charm.

Pleasure-seeking also tends to form habits that are hard to break. Like the morning coffee — a small pleasure at first, but soon, it feels like a pain when you don't have it. What once delighted you becomes something you depend on. Pleasure is like a spark: it lights you up for a moment, but fades quickly. It can lift your mood in the short term, but rarely offers the kind of happiness that truly lasts.

A deeper kind of happiness appears when you are fully involved in something you love doing. Instead of only watching football, you may decide to play the game yourself. In playing, you notice that you feel more energised and fully alive. Rather than just listening to music, you may choose to learn a musical instrument. As you create music, you notice a deeper connection with yourself and the activity. Instead of only eating a delicious dish prepared by someone else, you may find joy in cooking it yourself, especially when you prepare it for your family and friends. When you are fully engaged, you are not simply watching life — you are participating in it. You give your full attention, your effort, and your heart to the task.

At times like these, you enter a state where you forget the outside world and lose track of time. Psychologist Mihaly Csikszentmihalyi called this experience Flow. You feel a Flow state when there is a perfect balance between challenge and skill. If the task is too difficult, you feel stressed or anxious. If it is too easy, you feel bored. But when you meet the right challenge with the right skill, you find yourself deeply satisfied. Engagement asks for your time, patience, and learning. It may not always be instant, but once you find it, the happiness it brings is richer and longer-lasting than simple pleasure.

Yet, there is an even higher form of happiness — one that fills you with purpose. This is the happiness you feel when you contribute to something larger than yourself. You experience this kind of happiness when you do something that matters — not just to you, but to others too. You feel this when you give your time, your love, or your energy to make a positive difference, whether for one person or for many. This kind of happiness lasts much longer than pleasure or even engagement.

Professor Martin Seligman, a pioneer of positive psychology, once demonstrated this through a simple but powerful example. He took his students to a cinema and later asked them to rate how happy they felt. The following week, he took the same students to visit a community school, where they spent time playing with children from underprivileged backgrounds. Six months later, he asked them to recall both experiences. Most students could barely remember their trip to the cinema, but every single one of them remembered their visit to the school vividly. The happiness from that meaningful experience remained strong and fresh. When you serve others, you create happiness not only for them but also for yourself — and this happiness stays with you for years, sometimes even for life.

A real-life example of this is the story of Vinayak Lohani. In 2003, Vinayak was just twenty-five years old and had completed his studies at two of India's finest institutions — IIT Kharagpur and IIM Calcutta. Like many of his classmates, he could have easily secured a high-paying job and stepped into the corporate world. But Vinayak was listening to another voice — the voice of Swami Vivekananda, who called people to selfless service and to make their life one with those who suffer.

Vinayak chose a different path. He decided not to take up a corporate job. Instead, he started Parivaar, a home for destitute and abandoned children. He began with almost nothing — no funding, no team, and no grand strategy. He started with just three children in a small rented house on the outskirts of Kolkata. With faith, determination, and the desire to serve, he kept going. People who saw his sincerity slowly joined in — some gave money, others gave time, and some offered trust.

Today, Parivaar is one of India's largest free residential institutions for children from vulnerable backgrounds. Thousands of children now have a safe home, an education, and the warmth of a family because one young man dared to choose meaning over security. Vinayak's story shows you that you do not have to wait for the perfect opportunity. You do not need to be rich or fully prepared. You can begin exactly where you are — with love, courage, and the willingness to serve.

Now you can see that happiness is not just one thing. It is made of many layers. When you allow yourself simple pleasures, you brighten your day. When you engage deeply, you bring focus, fulfillment, and energy into your life. When you live with meaning, you create lasting happiness — not just for yourself, but for others too. You do not need to go searching for happiness.

You already have the power to create it, right where you are, with what you have. And you can start today.

In the end, the true measure of success is not just what you have achieved, but whether you are happy now. Real success is found in asking yourself, Am I happy today? and Are the actions I am taking leading me towards lasting happiness? You may find yourself at different stages of your life's journey, perhaps even facing struggles, challenges, or sacrifices. You may not always feel happy in every moment, especially if you are in the midst of the difficult stages of your story, like the hero who faces trials before reaching triumph. Yet, even when happiness seems distant, you can find strength in knowing that you are moving in the right direction. What you are doing has meaning. It is driven by a purpose larger than yourself.

You do not have to experience perfect happiness at every step. What matters is that you are consciously walking a path where pleasure, engagement, and meaning come together. When you align your life with this deeper purpose, you plant the seeds for lasting joy — not only for yourself, but for those you touch along the way.

Questions for reflection

- *What are some simple activities in your life that bring you joy? Do you make time for these pleasures regularly, or have they become habits that you no longer notice?*

- *Can you recall a moment when you were so involved in something that you lost track of time? What were you doing, and how did it feel?*

- *Are there areas in your life where you feel a sense of flow — where the challenge and your skills meet perfectly? How can you create more space for such moments?*

- *What activities or causes in your life give you a sense of deeper meaning or purpose? Are you making time for them?*

- *When you look at your current actions and choices, are they aligned with the kind of happiness you want in the long run?*

- *Are there moments in your life where you were struggling or sacrificing something, but knew it was worth it because it meant something to you?*

- *If happiness were your true measure of success, what would you start doing more of — and what would you let go of?*

References and Further Reading

Seligman, Martin E.P., Authentic Happiness: Using the New Positive Psychology to Realize Your Potential for Lasting Fulfillment, (Free Press, 2004)

Csikszentmihalyi, Mihaly, Flow: The Psychology of Optimal Experience, (Harper & Row, 1990)

Lyubomirsky, Sonja, The How of Happiness: A New Approach to Getting the Life You Want (Penguin Press, 2007)

Swami Sarvapriyananda at IITK: Happiness – Vedanta and Positive Psychology https://www.youtube.com/watch?v=JXUsxSX2QPI

Vinayak Lohani and Parivaar, https://parivaar.org

"Many of life's failures are people who did not realise how close they were to success when they gave up."
– Thomas Edison

CHAPTER 12

Ganbatte - Do Your Best, Keep Going

I am excited, eager, and nervous as I write this final chapter. Finishing the first draft of the book in fourteen days was a real challenge. It tested my discipline, resilience, and self-belief. I set out on this journey with a vision, pushing myself beyond my limits, determined to bring this book to life. As I write these final words, this journey reflects a larger story. It's about perseverance, not giving up, and fighting for dreams against all odds. This is like the overnight success stories we see on social media. The draft took less than 14 days to finish but involved over 20 years of preparation. That includes reading, thinking, discussing, and writing over 100 blogs and articles. Now, it is ready after many more days of revising, editing, and publishing.

I can assert that I cracked the code for success, which I can summarise in the Japanese philosophy of Ganbatte; it conveys the message: **Do your best, don't give up, and keep moving forward.**

Ganbatte is a popular Japanese phrase. It captures the spirit of perseverance, determination, and resilience. It's about moving ahead despite challenges. It values effort as a virtue and always aims for improvement.

In Japanese culture, 'Ganbatte' means more than motivation. It reflects the belief that hard work leads to growth and success. In academics, work, sports, or personal struggles, people say "Ganbatte!" to encourage each other. This shows that success comes from hard work and persistence, not quick results.

At its heart, Ganbatte is about moving forward despite obstacles. It reminds us that setbacks are part of the journey. Perseverance brings progress. We may not control the outcome, but we can control our effort and attitude. So, keep pushing forward, embrace challenges, and always strive for your best.

To capture the essence of this journey, Sylvester Gardenzio "Sly" Stallone stands out. His story of determination, struggle, and triumph is truly extraordinary. His rise from rejection to global fame shows what's possible when we refuse to give up. It highlights belief in ourselves, even when others don't, and the importance of pushing forward against the odds.

Most people know Sylvester Stallone as the Hollywood legend behind Rocky Balboa. They see his success, fame, and fortune. But many are unaware of the heart-wrenching journey that led him there.

Stallone was not born into privilege. He was not one of those actors who had a smooth ride to stardom. He was born with a partially paralysed face due to complications at birth, which caused his distinctive slurred speech and drooping lip. The traits that later made him unique were, in his early years, the reasons for his constant rejection.

Hollywood did not want him. Casting directors turned him down repeatedly, telling him he was not leading-man material. He was considered too rough, too awkward, too different. No one believed he could ever become a movie star.

His financial struggles were even worse. He was so broke that he had to sell his wife's jewellery to afford basic necessities. The bills kept stacking up. Soon, he hit rock bottom, standing outside a liquor store with his only friend—his beloved dog, Butkus. He had no choice but to sell Butkus for fifty dollars just to buy food. That moment, watching his best friend walk away with a stranger, was one of the lowest points of his life.

But even in the face of such despair, he refused to give up.

One night, Stallone watched a boxing match between Muhammad Ali and Chuck Wepner. Wepner, a surprising underdog, faced the greatest boxer ever. He took every punch but refused to fall. Something about that fight sparked something deep within him. He rushed home and, in a burst of creative energy, wrote the screenplay for Rocky in just three days.

With the script in hand, he went back to Hollywood, pitching it to every studio he could. And finally, people started to take notice. Studios loved the script, and they were ready to pay big money for it. They offered him $125,000, which was a fortune for someone struggling to get by.

But there was one condition: he could not play Rocky.

The studios wanted to cast a well-known actor, someone they believed could carry the film. Stallone was adamant. He refused to sell his script unless he played the lead.

People thought he was insane. Here he was, a starving actor turning down life-changing money. But for Stallone, money was not the goal—his dream was. He had written Rocky for himself, and if he let someone else take that role, he would be selling his soul.

The studios increased their offer to two hundred and fifty thousand dollars. Then three hundred and fifty thousand dollars. Still, he said no. Finally, after much back and forth, they agreed to let him play Rocky but only gave him thirty-five thousand dollars to make it happen.

And what was the first thing he did with that money?

He went straight back to that liquor store to buy back his dog. The man who had bought Butkus knew how much he meant to Stallone and demanded fifteen thousand dollars to return him. Stallone paid for it without hesitation. He got his best friend back, and they were in that fight together.

The filming of Rocky was far from glamorous. There were no big budgets, no extravagant sets, no luxury trailers. It was shot on a shoestring budget with a cast and crew who believed in the story just as much as he did. The fight scenes were rehearsed like real boxing matches because they could not afford multiple takes. The punches, the pain, the struggle—it was all real.

When Rocky hit the theatres, something incredible happened.

It did not just succeed. It exploded.

People resonated with the story of the underdog who refused to quit. Rocky became a worldwide hit. It won three Academy Awards, including Best Picture. This success turned Stallone from a struggling actor into a global icon.

But more than that, Rocky was not just a film. It was a reflection of his own journey. Just like Rocky Balboa, Stallone had been knocked down, underestimated, and told he was not good enough. And just like Rocky, he got back up, again and again, until he won.

Stallone's story is the embodiment of the Japanese philosophy of Ganbatte—the spirit of doing one's best, persevering no matter how hard things get, and of moving forward despite obstacles.

In Japan, Ganbatte is more than just a word; it is a way of life. It is the belief that effort itself is also valuable, along with one's commitment to a goal rather than immediate success. It is about pushing beyond limits, embracing struggle as part of the journey, and finding honour in perseverance.

Ganbatte does not promise that things will be easy. It does not guarantee success overnight. What it does promise is that those who refuse to give up, those who keep going despite setbacks, will find meaning and fulfillment in the journey towards success and fulfillment.

If you are facing challenges, if you feel like giving up, remember the Rocky story. Remember that success is not about how talented you are or how lucky you get. It is about resilience. It is about pushing through rejection, through failure, through the hardest of times, and never stopping.

The road to success will not be easy. There will be times when you will feel like quitting. But that is when you must remember this - Ganbatte !

Do your best. Keep moving. Do not give up.

Questions for reflection

- *When faced with setbacks, do you see them as signs to stop or challenges to overcome?*

- *What dream or goal have you been holding back on due to fear of failure or rejection?*

- *If success were measured by perseverance rather than results, how would you approach your work differently?*

- *What is one situation in your life where you can apply the Ganbatte mindset right now?*

- *How can you redefine failure as part of your journey rather than the end of it?*

References and Further Reading

Stallone, Sylvester. Sly Moves: My Proven Program to Lose Weight, Build Strength, Gain Willpower, and Live Your Dream. Harper Entertainment, 2005.

Pressfield, Steven. The War of Art: Break Through the Blocks and Win Your Inner Creative Battles. Black Irish Entertainment, 2002.

Duckworth, Angela. Grit: The Power of Passion and Perseverance. Scribner, 2016.

Clear, James. Atomic Habits: An Easy & Proven Way to Build Good Habits & Break Bad Ones. Avery, 2018.

Wagner, Albert Liebermann. Ganbatte: The Japanese Art of Always Moving Forward. Tuttle Publishing, 2021.

"We have two lives, and the second begins when we realise we only have one." – Mario de Andrade

Chapter 13

WHAT NEXT – Final Thoughts

We often live as if time is unlimited, postponing dreams and waiting for the right moment to truly live. Yet, compared to the vast history of the universe, our existence is just a fleeting moment. Within this short span, we chase achievements as if we are eternal, deferring joy and seeking validation that never seems to arrive. The reality is time does not wait. The second life begins when we recognise that this one is all we have—when we stop merely existing and start living with purpose, passion, and authenticity.

When Rishi Sunak became the Prime Minister of the United Kingdom, social media erupted with jokes. One of the most widely shared ones suggested that Sundar Pichai's father called Sundar and said, "See, Mr.Sunak's son became Prime Minister, and you are just the CEO of Google."

It's amusing because it reflects a reality you probably know well — no matter how much you achieve, someone will always find a way to remind you that you could have done more. You may have grown up chasing that one moment of approval — a word of recognition from your parents or partner, a nod from society, or validation from a mentor or peer or a friend. But the bar keeps shifting. Just when you expect to finally hear, "Well done" the target moves again.

But on the positive side, the absence of external approval makes many people drive for success. Some of the most impactful people in history never had the luxury of easy validation. They were not constantly told they were special, nor were they given undue praise. Instead, the absence of early recognition made them resilient, self-driven, and grounded. It made them push harder, not for applause but for the sheer pursuit of excellence. It is important to ge that that balance.

Ratan Tata, one of India's most respected industrialists, did not seek public validation when he decided to acquire international brands like Jaguar and Land Rover under the Tata Group. Many doubted whether Tata Motors could handle such an ambitious expansion. Even within the business community, some questioned his vision. But Ratan Tata was not motivated by proving others wrong—his mission was to build Indian businesses with global reach while maintaining a deep commitment to ethics and philanthropy. Today, his name is synonymous with integrity and leadership, not because he sought recognition but because he pursued impact.

Even with all your accomplishments, you might still feel like you haven't done enough. You hit milestone after milestone, take on more responsibility, push yourself harder — yet that deep craving for validation lingers. The challenge is, external validation is a moving target. No matter how much you achieve, there's always another level, another expectation, someone who's done just a little bit more.

At some point, if you truly want to create impact, you stop trying to impress others and start defining success on your own terms — often by focusing on how you contribute to others. Take the example of Ram Charan, the author of more than 20 business books, including the best-seller Execution: The Discipline of Getting Things Done. His journey is a reminder that lasting success often follows when you shift from seeking approval to serving meaningfully.

Ram Charan is a renowned business advisor, author, and consultant whose life has been marked by an unusual and highly disciplined existence. Unlike most successful corporate strategists, Charan has lived without a permanent home for decades, choosing instead to travel constantly to advise Fortune 500 CEOs, board members, and leaders across the globe.

Born in India, Charan pursued engineering before earning his MBA and doctorate from Harvard Business School, where he later became a professor. However, instead of settling into academia, he chose a life of continuous movement, living out of hotels and spending his time immersed in the world of business. His daily routine is focused purely on work—he does not own a home, avoids personal distractions, and dedicates himself completely to mentoring leaders and solving corporate challenges.

Charan's unique lifestyle allows him to be deeply embedded in the companies he advises, offering direct, no-nonsense advice that has earned him a reputation as one of the world's most influential business thinkers. His story is a testament to the idea that success does not always follow conventional paths. Instead of wealth or luxury, his fulfillment comes from his relentless focus on guiding others to make better business decisions. His existence is both mysterious and inspiring—a life devoted entirely to knowledge, strategy, and the pursuit of excellence in leadership.

It is worth taking a pause and asking—who are you still trying to impress?

Are you seeking validation from parents or teachers who may never openly express their pride?

Is it society that will always set new benchmarks?

Is it a rival whose recognition you secretly desire?

If the person you are trying to impress has the power to determine your happiness, then you may never feel truly fulfilled.

What if, instead of waiting for someone else to say, "I am proud of you," you said it to yourself?

What if success was not measured by external validation but by how deeply fulfilled you feel in what you do?

What if, instead of proving yourself to others, you focused on becoming the best version of yourself?

At some point in life, a decision must be made about whose opinion truly matters.

If one keeps waiting for others to acknowledge their worth, they may spend their entire life chasing approval that never comes. Success is not about proving something to others. It is about living a life that feels authentic and fulfilling.

When the need for external validation is released, something powerful happens. There is a shift from trying to meet expectations to simply enjoying what one does. The endless race for approval is replaced with purpose, passion, and joy.

If no one ever acknowledged your achievements, would they still be meaningful to you?

If the answer is yes, then you are already successful. If the answer is no, perhaps it is time to stop seeking validation and start embracing your own worth.

The only person you ever need to impress is yourself. You are already successful but you don't see it that way. You are enough. Most people think that they can help others once they achieve their goals, but the sense of being successful comes once you start helping others.

The shift begins once you move from operating with a "me" mindset to a "we" mindset. The ultimate goal is to support every individual on this planet in their journey towards self-realisation and to help them live a life of possibility.

My Soul Is in a Hurry

This is a poem by Mario de Andrade (São Paulo, 1893–1945), poet, writer, essayist, and musicologist. One of the founders of Brazilian modernism.

I counted my years and found that I have less time to live than I have ever lived.

I feel like this child who won a box of sweets: he eats the first ones with pleasure,

but when he realises there are only a few left, he truly begins to savour them.

I no longer have time for endless meetings where nothing is achieved.

I no longer have time to endure absurd people who, regardless of their age, have not grown.

I no longer have time to struggle with mediocrity.

I do not want to be in meetings where inflated egos march.

I do not tolerate manipulators and opportunists.

My time is too short to discuss trivialities.

I want the essentials because my soul is in a hurry.

I want to live with people who are real.

People who can laugh at their mistakes.

People who do not imagine their success.

People who defend human dignity and walk alongside truth and righteousness.

I want to surround myself with people who know how to touch the hearts of others.

People who, through the hard blows of life, have learned to grow with the gentle touches of the soul.

Yes, I am in a hurry—to live with the intensity that only maturity can bring.

I do not want to waste any of the sweets I have left.

I am sure they will be more delicious than those I have already eaten.

My goal is to reach the end contentedly, in peace with myself, my loved ones, and my conscience.

We have two lives, and the second begins when we realise we only have one.

Questions for reflection

- *If no one were watching and there was no need for approval, what would you pursue with passion?*

- *Who or what has been shaping your definition of success, and is it truly aligned with what matters to you?*

- *What would your life look like if you stopped seeking validation and started living authentically?*

- *Where in your life are you holding back because of fear—fear of judgment, failure, or not being "enough"?*

- *If today were the last day you had to prove yourself to anyone, how would you choose to live moving forward?*

References and Further Reading

Books

Charan, Ram. Execution: The Discipline of Getting Things Done. Crown Business, 2002.

A practical guide on turning strategies into results, co-authored with Larry Bossidy, former CEO of Honeywell.

Christensen, Clayton M. How Will You Measure Your Life? Harper Business, 2012.

Explores how personal values, purpose, and impact define true success beyond career achievements.

Covey, Stephen R. The 7 Habits of Highly Effective People: Powerful Lessons in Personal Change. Free Press, 1989.

A timeless guide to building strong personal and professional habits for long-term success and fulfilment.

Harari, Yuval Noah. 21 Lessons for the 21st Century. Spiegel & Grau, 2018.

Examines how artificial intelligence, automation, and societal change will shape the future and the human role within it.

Articles & Reports

Colvin, Geoff. "The Strange Existence of Ram Charan." Fortune Magazine, April 30, 2007. https://money.cnn.com/magazines/fortune/fortune_archive/2007/04/30/8405482/index.htm

Explores the unconventional life and work ethic of Ram Charan, one of the world's most sought-after business advisors.

Jobs, Steve. "You Can't Connect the Dots Looking Forward." Stanford University Commencement Address, 2005.

A legendary speech on embracing uncertainty and trusting that your passions and experiences will shape your future.

Musk, Elon. "The Future of AI: A Threat or an Opportunity?" MIT AI Conference, 2017.

Discusses the ethical and existential risks of artificial intelligence and the need for responsible innovation.

Poetry & Philosophy

De Andrade, Mario. "My Soul is in a Hurry."

A poetic reflection on the urgency of living fully, focusing on depth, purpose, and human connection.

Vivekananda, Swami. Arise, Awake, and Stop Not Till the Goal is Reached.

A call for self-realisation, resilience, and purposeful living in the face of external pressures.

ANNEXURES (REFERENCE MATERIAL)

Timelss Models, frameworks, and philosophies to support your transformation

> *"The reality is that you will grieve forever. You will not 'get over' the loss of a loved one; you will learn to live with it. You will heal, and you will rebuild yourself around the loss you have suffered."*
> — *Elisabeth Kübler-Ross.*

The Kübler-Ross Grief Curve

Understanding Change, Loss, and Transformation

Introduction

Grief is a universal human experience, one that touches everyone at some point in their lives. Whether it is the death of a loved one, the end of a relationship, the loss of a job, or a major life transition, grief takes many forms. The Kübler-Ross Grief Curve is one of the most well-known psychological models that describes how individuals navigate loss and change. Originally developed to explain how terminally ill patients cope with their diagnosis, this model has since been widely applied to a variety of personal and professional situations.

This chapter explores the origins of the Kübler-Ross model, its five stages, and its broader applications in understanding not only grief but also any significant life change. It also discusses variations of the model and the criticisms it has received over time. By understanding this framework, individuals can better navigate their own emotional responses and support others through their journeys of loss and transformation.

The Origins of the Kübler-Ross Grief Curve

The Kübler-Ross model was introduced by Swiss-American psychiatrist Elisabeth Kübler-Ross in her 1969 book On Death and Dying. Born in Switzerland in 1926, Kübler-Ross trained as a psychiatrist and later moved to the United States, where she worked extensively with terminally ill patients. Her interest in death and the psychological responses to it developed after witnessing the suffering of concentration camp survivors during World War II and later through her work with dying patients in hospitals.

During the 1960s, death and dying were rarely discussed openly in medical and psychological fields. Kübler-Ross challenged this silence by interviewing hundreds of patients facing terminal diagnoses. She sought to understand how they processed their emotions and coped with the reality of their mortality. Through these interviews, she identified a pattern of emotional responses that most patients experienced, which she later categorised into five distinct stages of grief.

Initially, the model was designed to help healthcare professionals and families support dying patients. However, over time, it became clear that these emotional stages applied far beyond terminal illness. Today, the Kübler-Ross model is widely used in counselling, psychology, organisational change management, and personal development.

The Five Stages of Grief

The Kübler-Ross Grief Curve outlines five stages that individuals commonly experience when dealing with loss or profound change. It is important to note that these stages do not always occur in a fixed order, nor do all individuals experience every stage. Grief is a deeply personal process, and people may move back and forth between stages or experience them simultaneously.

Denial

The first stage of grief is denial, where individuals struggle to accept the reality of their loss. This stage acts as a psychological defence mechanism, allowing the person to process overwhelming emotions at a more manageable pace.

Someone who has just lost a loved one may continue to expect them to walk through the door. A person who has been made redundant may insist that they will be reinstated.

Denial can take the form of shock, disbelief, or avoidance. It allows individuals to create temporary emotional distance from painful realities. While it may seem unhelpful, denial serves a protective function by preventing people from becoming emotionally overwhelmed too quickly.

Anger

As denial begins to fade, it is often replaced by anger. The reality of the situation starts to set in, and individuals look for someone or something to blame. They may feel anger towards themselves, others, or even fate. This stage can manifest as frustration, resentment, or bitterness.

A bereaved individual might feel angry at the medical team for not doing enough or at their loved one for leaving them. Someone experiencing a relationship breakdown may blame their former partner or feel anger towards themselves for past mistakes. Anger is a natural response to loss and serves as a way of expressing the pain that denial had previously shielded them from.

Bargaining

The third stage, bargaining, is characterised by an attempt to negotiate or regain control over the situation. Individuals may dwell on "if only" statements, reflecting on what they could have done differently to prevent the loss. A person facing a terminal illness might promise to change their lifestyle in exchange for more time. Someone going through a divorce may desperately try to reconcile, believing they can undo the damage.

Bargaining is often accompanied by feelings of guilt and regret. Individuals may wish they had acted differently or tried to make deals with a higher power, hoping to reverse the outcome. This stage reflects a deep desire to restore a sense of control over an uncontrollable situation.

Depression

As bargaining proves futile, the person enters the depression stage. This phase involves deep sadness, hopelessness, and withdrawal from daily activities. The full weight of the loss is now undeniable, and the individual may feel overwhelmed by emotions.

This stage is often the longest and most challenging, as it requires people to sit with their pain rather than resist it. Symptoms can include lethargy, loss of motivation, and emotional numbness. It is important to differentiate between grief-related depression, which is a natural response to loss, and clinical depression, which may require professional intervention.

Acceptance

In the final stage, the individual reaches a level of acceptance. This does not mean they are happy with what has happened, but rather that they have made peace with reality. They begin to integrate the loss into their lives and move forward with a renewed sense of purpose.

Acceptance allows for healing and growth. While the pain of loss may never fully disappear, individuals find ways to adapt and continue living meaningful lives. They may establish new routines, develop new perspectives, or even find a sense of purpose through their experiences.

Variations and Criticisms of the Kübler-Ross Model

Over the years, many psychologists and grief counsellors have expanded on Kübler-Ross's work. Some have suggested that grief is more fluid than the five stages imply.

One alternative model is the Dual Process Model of Grief, which argues that people oscillate between experiencing their grief and engaging in everyday life. Another variation is the Seven Stages of Grief, which includes additional stages such as shock and reconstruction.

Critics argue that the Kübler-Ross model oversimplifies grief and suggests a rigid progression. In reality, grief is highly individualised, and not everyone experiences these stages in order or at all. Despite these critiques, the model remains widely recognised as a useful framework for understanding emotional responses to loss and change.

Applying the Kübler-Ross Model to Personal and Organisational Change

While originally focused on end-of-life care, the Kübler-Ross model is now applied in many contexts. In workplace change management, it helps leaders understand employees' reactions to restructures, redundancies, or major shifts in company culture. In personal development, it is used to navigate transitions such as career changes, breakups, or relocations.

Understanding these emotional stages can help individuals manage their own responses to change while also offering support to others who may be struggling.

Conclusion

The Kübler-Ross Grief Curve provides a valuable framework for understanding loss, change, and emotional processing. Although it is not a rigid or universal experience, it helps to normalise the range of emotions people face during difficult transitions.

Whether applied to grief, personal transformation, or professional challenges, the model serves as a reminder that healing is a journey. Acceptance does not mean forgetting; it means finding a way to move forward while carrying the lessons of the past.

"A hero is someone who has given his or her life to something bigger than oneself." – Joseph Cambell.

The Hero's Journey

The Hero's Journey, a concept popularised by Joseph Campbell, is a timeless narrative pattern found in myths, legends, and modern storytelling. It represents the universal human experience of growth, transformation, and self-discovery.

At its core, the Hero's Journey follows a three-act structure:

Departure – The hero is called to adventure, often leaving behind the familiar world.

Initiation – They face trials, mentors, and inner struggles, ultimately transforming through challenges.

Return – The hero comes back, bringing newfound wisdom and change to their world.

From ancient myths to modern films like Star Wars, The Lord of the Rings, and Harry Potter, this journey reflects our personal struggles and the pursuit of purpose. As Campbell famously said: "The cave you fear to enter holds the treasure you seek."

The 12 Stages of the Hero's Journey

1. The Ordinary World – Life Before the Journey

Every hero starts in an ordinary world, where life is predictable and comfortable. However, beneath the surface, there is often a feeling of restlessness or dissatisfaction. You may feel like something is missing, but you are unsure what it is. This is the stage where many people remain stuck, waiting for something to change.

2. Call to Adventure – A Challenge Appears

A defining moment disrupts life as usual. This could be an opportunity, a new challenge, or a sudden realisation that things need to change. The call to adventure can be external, such as a job loss or a life-altering event, or internal, such as an overwhelming desire for something more.

3. Refusal of the Call – Resistance and Fear

At first, the hero resists. Fear of failure, self-doubt, or the comfort of familiarity holds them back. They may convince themselves that they are not ready or that the timing is not right. Many people stay in this phase for years, afraid to step outside their comfort zones.

4. Meeting the Mentor – Guidance Arrives

At this stage, a mentor, coach, or inspiring figure appears to offer wisdom and encouragement. The mentor does not do the work for the hero but provides insight, tools, and motivation. This guidance can come from a teacher, a book, a friend, or even an experience that shifts perspective.

5. Crossing the First Threshold – Leaving the Comfort Zone

The hero makes a decision to step into the unknown. This is the first real commitment to change, the point where there is no turning back. It might be starting a new job, moving to a different city, launching a business, or making a significant lifestyle shift.

6. Tests, Allies, and Enemies – Facing Challenges

Once the hero enters the new world, they face a series of challenges. Along the way, they gain allies who support their journey and encounter obstacles that test their resilience. This stage is about learning, adapting, and overcoming initial setbacks.

7. Approach to the Inmost Cave – The Final Preparation

The hero gets closer to their goal, but before the ultimate test, they must confront their inner doubts and limitations. This stage is often marked by deep reflection, self-questioning, and a critical turning point where the hero must decide if they are truly ready to transform.

8. The Ordeal – The Greatest Challenge

The hero faces their most difficult test yet. This could be a major failure, a loss, or a moment of extreme pressure that forces them to push beyond their limits. Many people quit at this stage, but those who persevere gain incredible strength and wisdom.

9. Reward (Seizing the Sword) – The Breakthrough

After overcoming the ordeal, the hero is rewarded. This may come in the form of personal growth, a new opportunity, or the realisation that they are stronger than they ever imagined. It is the moment when everything starts to make sense.

10. The Road Back – Returning to Reality

Even after the breakthrough, the journey is not over. The hero must now integrate their growth into daily life. They may face resistance from those who expect them to remain the same or struggle with the transition from their extraordinary journey back to routine life.

11. Resurrection – *The Final Test*

Before the transformation is complete, there is one final challenge. This is the ultimate test to prove that the hero has truly changed. It requires them to apply everything they have learned to a real-world situation.

12. Return with the Elixir – *A New Beginning*

The hero returns home, transformed. They bring back wisdom, new skills, and a greater sense of purpose. Their journey is now complete, and they are ready to share their insights with others and continue growing in new ways.

"Choose a job you love, and you will never have to work a day in your life." — *Confucius.*

Ikigai

The Philosophy of a Meaningful Life

Introduction

In a world that is increasingly driven by achievement, productivity, and financial success, many people find themselves questioning the deeper meaning of their lives. Why do we work so hard? What makes life fulfilling? Is there a way to align our daily activities with our passions and purpose? The Japanese concept of Ikigai, which translates to "reason for being," provides a profound answer to these questions.

Rooted in the culture of Okinawa, Japan, a region known for having one of the highest populations of centenarians in the world, Ikigai is not merely about financial success or professional growth. Instead, it represents the delicate balance between passion, mission, vocation, and profession—a holistic approach to life that integrates what we love, what we are good at, what the world needs, and what we can be paid for.

Unlike the Western idea of retirement, where people work until they no longer have to, the Okinawan elders continue to engage in meaningful activities, finding joy in work, community, and personal pursuits well into their 80s, 90s, and even 100s. This sense of purpose is believed to be one of the key reasons for their longevity, happiness, and overall well-being.

Understanding Ikigai: A Life of Purpose and Joy

The Ikigai framework is often represented as a Venn diagram with four intersecting circles:

1. What you love (Passion) – Activities that bring you joy and fulfilment.

2. What you are good at (Skills/Talents) – The unique strengths and abilities that set you apart.

3. What the world needs (Mission) – How your work or contributions can positively impact others.

4. What you can be paid for (Profession/Vocation) – The practical aspect of financial sustainability.

At the centre of these four elements lies Ikigai, the sweet spot where personal satisfaction and societal contribution merge. Unlike a career-focused or profit-driven approach, Ikigai encourages a life-oriented perspective, integrating work, passion, and purpose into a harmonious existence.

Why Ikigai Matters in Today's World

Many people spend their entire lives in jobs they dislike, living on autopilot, simply working for a paycheck and counting down the days to the weekend. This approach often leads to burnout, stress, and a lack of fulfilment. In contrast, people who have discovered their Ikigai find themselves excited to wake up every morning because their work aligns with their values and passion.

The Modern Dilemma: Success Without Fulfillment

Consider the story of John, a successful investment banker. He had a high-paying job, prestige, and financial security, yet he felt empty inside. His work was demanding, stressful, and disconnected from his personal passions. Every Sunday night, he felt an overwhelming sense of dread thinking about the week ahead.

John decided to reevaluate his life. Through deep introspection, he realised that his true passion had always been mentoring and coaching young professionals. After several months of exploring his interests, he transitioned into a career in leadership coaching, merging his financial expertise with his love for teaching. Today, he earns well while doing something he genuinely enjoys. His life is not just about making money but about helping others grow—a shift that has given him a renewed sense of purpose and happiness.

Ikigai and Longevity: Lessons from Okinawa

The people of Okinawa, Japan, have been studied extensively for their exceptionally long and healthy lives. Researchers attribute their longevity to several factors, including a plant-based diet, strong social connections, and an active lifestyle. However, one of the most significant factors is their deep sense of purpose—Ikigai.

Unlike in Western cultures, where retirement often marks a slowdown in life, Okinawans do not have a word for "retirement". Instead, they believe in having a lifelong purpose—whether it is tending to a garden, teaching younger generations, or practising a craft. Their daily routines are filled with small joys and meaningful interactions, which contribute to their overall mental, emotional, and physical well-being.

A famous example is Dr Shigeaki Hinohara, a Japanese doctor who continued practising medicine until he was 105 years old. He believed that having a sense of purpose and curiosity about life was essential for longevity. He saw patients daily, wrote books, and gave lectures well into his later years. His Ikigai was to serve others, and he lived a vibrant, energetic life because of it.

Applying Ikigai in Everyday Life

Finding Ikigai is not about making drastic changes overnight. It is a gradual process of self-reflection, exploration, and intentional living. Here are some ways to start applying Ikigai in daily life:

Identify What Brings You Joy

Think about what excites you, what you would do even if you weren't paid, and what activities make you lose track of time. These are clues to your passions.

Recognise Your Strengths

Assess your natural talents, skills, and experiences. What are you exceptionally good at? Where do others seek your guidance? These strengths can become an integral part of your vocation or profession.

Contribute to Something Larger Than Yourself

True fulfilment comes from helping others. Identify how your skills and passions can serve a greater purpose. Whether through your career, community work, or personal projects, making a positive impact brings lasting happiness.

Integrate Ikigai Into Your Work

If your current job does not align with your Ikigai, find ways to incorporate elements of it. This could mean shifting roles, starting a side project, or gradually transitioning into a new field that better matches your values.

Embrace the Journey, Not Just the Destination

Ikigai is not about achieving a single goal but about living with purpose every day. It's about finding beauty in daily routines, appreciating small joys, and continuously growing.

Conclusion

Ikigai is more than a philosophy; it is a way of life that encourages us to find joy and purpose in everything we do. It is the key to a balanced and fulfilling existence—one where work, passion, and contribution intersect. In a world that often prioritises success over well-being, Ikigai serves as a powerful reminder that true happiness comes not from what we achieve but from how we live each day.

Whether through our careers, relationships, or personal growth, embracing Ikigai allows us to wake up each morning with enthusiasm, knowing that our lives have meaning and purpose.

References and Further Reading on Ikigai

Several books have explored Ikigai in depth, making it accessible to a global audience.

"Ikigai: The Japanese Secret to a Long and Happy Life" – Héctor García and Francesc Miralles provide insights from Okinawan elders and practical steps for applying Ikigai to daily life.

"Awakening Your Ikigai" – Ken Mogi outlines the five pillars of Ikigai and how they influence happiness and well-being.

"The Little Book of Ikigai" – Ken Mogi further expands on how small habits and mindfulness contribute to a purposeful life.

"Ikigai for Business Leaders" – Tim Tamashiro explores how leaders can integrate Ikigai principles into work and management.

"At the center of your being, you have the answer; you know who you are, and you know what you want." – Lao Tzu

Ontology

The Study of Being

Ontology is one of the oldest and most fundamental branches of philosophy. It is concerned with the nature of existence, reality, and how entities are classified within the structure of the world. The term originates from the Greek words ontos, meaning 'being', and logos, meaning 'study' or 'discourse'. It is a discipline that seeks to understand what it means for something to exist and how different categories of being relate to one another. This field should not be confused with Oncology, which is the study of cancer, or Oenology, which is the study of wine, though the similarity in pronunciation has often led to humorous mix-ups.

Historically, ontology has its roots in the work of ancient philosophers, particularly Aristotle, who explored the classification of things in his work Categories. Aristotle laid the groundwork for understanding how entities can be grouped based on their essential properties. He identified primary substances—individual things such as a particular horse or a specific tree—and secondary substances, which refer to broader categories like 'horse' or 'tree'. His work in defining the structure of existence influenced centuries of philosophical thought and continues to shape modern discussions on the subject.

In contemporary philosophy, ontology has evolved into a discipline that intersects with various fields, including linguistics, artificial intelligence, and personal development. One of its modern applications, particularly in leadership and coaching, has been brought to the forefront by Werner Erhard. Through his work in personal transformation and the Landmark Forum, Erhard made the ontological approach accessible to the general public, demonstrating how an understanding of being can lead to profound personal and professional change.

In addition to its philosophical implications, ontology has found a practical application in the field of computer science. In artificial intelligence and data science, ontologies are used to define structured relationships between concepts and entities. These structured frameworks allow machines to process and interpret information in a way that mimics human reasoning. Ontological structures are fundamental to the development of knowledge graphs, semantic search engines, and machine learning algorithms.

For instance, Google's Knowledge Graph, which enhances search engine capabilities, relies on ontological frameworks to link information. Similarly, IBM Watson and other artificial intelligence systems use ontologies to refine their understanding of language and context. These applications illustrate how the study of being has transitioned from an abstract philosophical concept to a crucial component of modern technological advancements.

Werner Erhard is widely recognised for his work in personal development and transformational leadership. His contribution to ontology is not in the realm of academic philosophy but rather in making its principles practical for everyday life. In the 1970s, Erhard developed EST (Erhard Seminars Training), which later evolved into the Landmark Forum, a series of programmes designed to help individuals explore their way of being and shift their perspectives.

Erhard's approach to ontology emphasises that individuals are not merely defined by their circumstances or past experiences but by the way they 'are' in the world. He argued that language is not merely a tool for describing reality but is, in fact, generative—it creates reality. By changing one's language and thought patterns, a person can transform their experience of life. This perspective aligns with the later philosophy of Ludwig Wittgenstein, who suggested that the limits of language are the limits of one's world.

The ontological framework presented by Erhard suggests that individuals operate within certain 'ways of being' that are often invisible to them. These ways of being shape their actions, relationships, and overall engagement with life. By recognising and shifting these fundamental ways of being, individuals can open new possibilities for leadership, performance, and fulfilment. This approach has been widely adopted in coaching, leadership training, and organisational development.

The ontological approach shares significant similarities with the methodology presented in The Inner Game of Tennis by Tim Gallwey. While Gallwey's work is rooted in sports psychology, its implications extend far beyond athletic performance. His central idea is that individuals often create unnecessary mental interference that prevents them from performing at their best. By shifting focus from self-judgment to awareness and presence, individuals can achieve higher levels of effectiveness.

Like Erhard's ontological coaching, Gallwey's methodology is based on the idea that transformation is not about acquiring new techniques but about removing mental obstacles that prevent natural excellence. Both approaches highlight the importance of language, internal dialogue, and shifting perception to unlock potential. This alignment suggests that ontology, whether applied in leadership or in sports, has universal implications for personal growth and human performance.

The influence of ontology extends beyond philosophy and personal development into various domains in modern society. In leadership and executive coaching, ontological methodologies are used to help individuals and organisations navigate complex challenges. Many leadership programmes incorporate Erhard's principles, emphasising self-awareness, authenticity, and the power of language in shaping organisational culture.

In psychology and performance coaching, the concepts introduced by Tim Gallwey are now applied in fields such as mindfulness, cognitive behavioural therapy, and executive coaching. The recognition that one's internal state affects external performance has led to the widespread adoption of these ideas in corporate settings, sports training, and personal development initiatives.

In the realm of artificial intelligence and data science, ontological frameworks continue to be a foundation for structuring and categorising information. AI-driven systems that rely on ontologies are now essential in industries ranging from healthcare to finance, enabling more intelligent data processing and decision-making.

Ontology also plays a crucial role in education and learning sciences. Adaptive learning platforms, which personalise education based on student behaviour, use ontological structures to tailor content and optimise learning experiences. The application of ontological distinctions in pedagogy allows for more effective teaching methodologies and improved student outcomes.

Ontology, the study of being, has evolved from its ancient philosophical roots into a discipline with vast modern applications. From Aristotle's classification of existence to Wittgenstein's exploration of language and reality, the study of being has shaped human thought for centuries. In contemporary society, ontology is not only a subject of academic inquiry but a practical tool for leadership, coaching, artificial intelligence, and performance science.

Werner Erhard's contribution to ontology has made the concept of 'being' accessible to a wider audience, enabling individuals to transform their lives through self-awareness and language. His approach parallels the insights of Tim Gallwey, demonstrating that true excellence arises from removing internal barriers rather than merely acquiring external techniques.

As ontology continues to influence fields such as technology, business, and psychology, its relevance in shaping the human experience becomes ever more apparent. Whether in the context of AI-driven decision-making or personal transformation, the principles of being remain fundamental to understanding and engaging with the world. The study of ontology, far from being an abstract philosophical pursuit, offers valuable insights that can be applied in everyday life to enhance clarity, effectiveness, and overall well-being.

References and Further Reading on Ontology

Erhard, Werner, Michael C. Jensen, and Steve Zaffron. Being a Leader and the Effective Exercise of Leadership: An Ontological/Phenomenological Model. SSRN, 2008.

Zaffron, Steve, and Dave Logan. The Three Laws of Performance: Rewriting the Future of Your Organization and Your Life. Jossey-Bass, 2009.

Olalla, Julio. From Knowledge to Wisdom: Essays on the Crisis in Contemporary Learning. Newfield Network, 2004.

Gallwey, W. Timothy. The Inner Game of Tennis: The Classic Guide to the Mental Side of Peak Performance. Random House, 1974.

Kofman, Fred. Conscious Business: How to Build Value Through Values. Sounds True, 2006.

Closing:

Acknowledgements and the Author's Journey

"Feeling gratitude and not expressing it is like wrapping a present and not giving it." – William Arthur Ward

Acknowledgements

I would like to sincerely thank my family, friends, coaches, teachers, collaborators, and customers for their trust and support throughout my journey.

First and foremost, thank you to you, the reader. If this book inspires even one person to take meaningful action, then my purpose in writing it is fulfilled.

To my beloved parents—Dr Mohan Mithare, who showed me the power of working with quiet dedication and passion, never complaining, always contributing; and Malathi Mithare, whose kindness, love, and generosity taught me the deep joy that lies in helping others—thank you for being the foundation of everything I am.

I'm deeply grateful to my wife, partner, and friend, Veena, for her unwavering support, unconditional love, and for keeping me grounded in what truly matters. Our daughter, Nishka—with her creativity, diligence, and curiosity—continually inspires me to pursue what I love.

Thank you to my sister, Prafulla, and her family—Rajkumar and Soham Kalghatagi; to my brother, Rajesh Mithare, along with Amita, Siddhanth, and Mehek. My cousin, Ajay Mithare, has been a steady source of encouragement and understanding.

I'm thankful for the blessings and kindness of my in-laws, Jagannath and Veda Shetty, and for the warmth and presence of Vinay Shetty, Sarosh Hegde, and their sons, Vayun and Aatharv.

To Bhaskar Natarajan—mentor, coach, and friend—thank you for your belief in me, your insights, and your unwavering support.

To my school friends—my global, extended family—Guru Mummigatti, Rakesh Honnaputmath, Shrikanth Halenayak, Subodh Koperde, Ravi Kulkarni, Rajkumar Noubade, Kumar Sullikeri, Vilas Goudar, Rajeev S, Manjunath Doddamani, Mukund Mohan, Sanjay Amminbhavi, Mallikarjun Tuppad, Anil Rokhade, Kiran Patil, Raju Patil, Asif Jamakhandi, and Santosh Gadkar—thank you for being a constant presence in my life.

Special thanks to all friends who reviewed early drafts and offered valuable feedback.

I'm grateful to Krishna Kishore Kommu—my guide and friend—and to our ProcessWhirl core team, Vijetha and Ajetha, for your trust and energy.

To Natasha Custon, thank you for your optimism, kindness, and for our collaboration in learning the Being a Leader model.

To Paul Darnell—your trust and encouragement helped me rediscover momentum. I'm also thankful to the 3S Knowledge team: Gireesh, Manoj, Ravi, Saurabh, Amarendra, and Sophie.

Sri Katte—thank you for your creativity, your faith in me, and for being the very first student of WHAT NEXT.

Deep appreciation to Savitha SR for supporting me through difficult times and for encouraging me to relaunch WHAT NEXT. And to Manikanth L B, for your deep trust and thoughtful conversations.

Nishal William Tellis—thank you for always helping me find the right book at the right moment. Sven Ihnken—your clarity, questions, and companionship have been both grounding and energising.

To former line managers who became mentors and friends—V Subramanyam (VSM), Ruchi Kapoor, and Jyoti Bhat—thank you for your continued support.

To the many thought leaders and coaches who have shaped my thinking—Navneet Bhushan, Hari Srinivasan, Tataghat Verma, Pradeep Soundararajan, Raghuram Kote, and Sai Ramesh (MCC)—thank you.

To my coach brothers, Satyanarayan Kumar and Arijit Mitra—your friendship and encouragement have meant more than words can express.

Manjunath Rao BV—thank you for introducing me to Covey's 7 Habits many years ago, for your unconditional support, and for helping me settle in when I first moved to the UK.

Dr Manish Kumar—thank you for always making time to explore ideas and for helping me expand my YouTube reach in such creative ways.

To Shilpa Sikotra, Meghana K, and Jackie McKinley—thank you for our meaningful conversations around J. Krishnamurti's teachings. BK Geetha—thank you for lighting the way with Monday meditations and your kind blessings.

To my dear friends Debabrata (Deb) and Schini Sil De, and their children, Ruku and Renne—thank you for your warmth, love, and unwavering support. Sudarshan Kallikeri, and Nagendra and Nimmi—thank you for your friendship and kindness.

Thanks to Satish Kadu, Kris Puthcode, Purvi Thakkar, Rishikesh Kardile, and Priyank Nandan for your encouragement and perspective.

To Shantala Matti Rao—your insight into the meaning of identity and the power of my name made a lasting impression.

To the many friends who have walked with me on this journey—Shylaja Siddappa, Vinay Haliyal, Rakesh Dev, Prakash Hegde, Krishna Murthy Malayian, Amogh Joshi, Dominic Clark-Abdullah, Carol Roche, Kam Zaman, Satheesh (KP), Babu Ramanathan, Sandeep Patil, Amit Patil, Unmesh Kulkarni, Anand Jayraman, Venkat Rao, Puneet Magan, Lavan Pinto, Krishna Chodipalli, Rolex, Nadir Talai, Sohil Ali, Bala, Paul Meridith, Aravind, Brindha Kalyanraman, Simmi, Anup, Swati Garg, Neelambari Shirodkar, Padmashree Deepak, Divya Sareen, Miguel Pereira, and Mohammed Rowther—thank you for your continued belief in me.

To the Agile coaching community—Tobias Mayer, Koren Stark, Natasha Baisiwala, Oscar Styf, Neeraj Clarke, Mike Crook, Nick Perry, Paul Witts, and Sanches Clark—thank you for your wisdom, support, and shared vision.

To all the students of the WHAT NEXT programme—you are the reason I do what I do. Your courage and openness continue to inspire me.

And to the many teachers, thinkers, and role models whose work has guided me—Swami Sarvapriyananda, Werner Erhard, Sridhar Vembu, Dr Pramod Verma, Stephen Covey, David Allen, Steve Jobs, Ray Dalio, Tony Robbins, Siddharth Rajsekar, Sadhguru, Jack Ma, Brian Chesky, Peter Drucker, Srikumar Rao, Ram Charan, Hermann Hesse, Bertrand Russell, Rumi, Prakash Iyer, and many more.

Special thanks to Shrikant Halanak for your constant support, especially when I needed it the most. To Rajkumar Noubade and Subodh Koparde for visiting and reminding me of what I'm capable of. Rajesh Honnapurmath—thank you for your unconditional support, your philosophical insight, and the wonderful book you gifted me, which helped spark and shape the design of this book. Ravi Kulkarni, Mallikarjun Tuppad, and Rajesh Honnapurmath—thank you for always making it a point to meet for dinner whenever I visit, despite your busy schedules. Your presence and warmth mean a great deal to me.

Initially, I wasn't planning to name anyone, fearing I might leave someone out. But I've come to believe it's better to risk forgetting a few than to withhold thanks from those I do remember. If I've missed your name, please know it wasn't intentional—you are deeply appreciated.

Being out of work gave me the time—and the quiet—to write this book. As Steve Jobs once said: "You can't connect the dots looking forward; you can only connect them looking backward." I now see how those dots have connected.

With gratitude,

Raghavendra Mithare

14 February 2025

Cheam / London, UK

"When you want something, all the universe conspires in helping you to achieve it."-Paulo Coelho, The Alchemist

My Journey

Different worlds shaped my early years—each one leaving its quiet imprint. I was born in Karwar, a small coastal town in southern India, and later moved to the rural villages of North Karnataka. These inland communities, though rich in spirit, had limited access to quality education. My father served as a General Practitioner (GP) in the government health service, much like the NHS in the UK. He was transferred from one village to another, mostly in North Karnataka, in and around Dharwad. It was in these modest surroundings that my journey of intellectual and philosophical exploration quietly began—nurtured by stories, lessons, and experiences that shaped the way I saw life.

Even with modest means, our life felt full. We were a typical middle-class family—not wealthy, but surrounded by respect and warmth. The villagers treated us with great affection, often assuming we were far wealthier than we actually were. Life among poor farmers had its own richness. At home, there was a quiet sense of 'enough'. My parents, sister, and brother cared for me deeply. Much of my early learning happened through home-schooling, which nurtured an independent approach to education—one that continues to guide me to this day.

Early exposure to Amar Chitra Katha tales—especially the stories of Tenali Rama—left a deep impression. In one tale, the goddess offers Tenali Rama a choice between wealth and knowledge. He chooses both, saying one is meaningless without the other. But his choice brings a divine curse, turning him into a Vidushaka, a jester. That paradox taught me that both wealth and wisdom matter—and so does the respect that holds them in balance.

Pillars of ancient wisdom, the Ramayana and Mahabharata deeply influenced how I see the world. Far beyond myth or legend, they offered profound insights into ethics, leadership, and the complexity of human nature. These epics taught me about the weight of responsibility, the challenges of decision-making, and the ongoing quest to live in alignment with dharma—one's true path. We moved from place to place, and eventually settled in Dharwad for my secondary schooling.

A turning point came when I first encountered Transactional Analysis and Gestalt Therapy during my school years. These ideas awakened a deep curiosity about the human mind. One story from Born to Win has stayed with me—the eagle raised among chickens, unaware of its true nature until it soared. It taught me a lifelong lesson: that within every person lies extraordinary potential, often hidden, waiting for the right moment to rise.

I was drawn to computer graphics, which led me to pursue a degree in Computer Science Engineering. Although graphics was just one subject in the final year, it initially captured my imagination. Over time, I became more passionate about Software Engineering—the art and science of building great software.

To deepen my understanding, I completed a Master of Technology in Software Engineering from the University of Mysore. I loved the experience—staying in a hostel, surrounded by friends, made that phase of life unforgettable.

A major turning point came when I learned Siddha Samadhi Yoga from Rishi Prabhakar. It taught me meditation, healthy eating, energy management, and the value of meaningful conversation. Practices like meditation and pranayama (breath control) have brought clarity and calm, especially in stressful times. They remain my go-to tools for inner stability.

I was fortunate to begin my career in the late 1990s, during a time of explosive growth in India's IT industry. I moved to Bangalore for my first job. Early on, I worked on large transformation projects and led teams to deliver real business value. A major milestone was being part of the team that achieved the world's first Level 5 rating in the Capability Maturity Model.

The 7 Habits of Highly Effective People by Stephen Covey opened the door to personal growth for me, planting the seeds of leadership and self-mastery. Later, Getting Things Done by David Allen gave me practical tools for productivity and efficiency.

The Alchemist by Paulo Coelho moved me deeply. Its message—that the universe supports those who follow their dreams—strengthened my belief that unseen forces guide us. Vision 2020 by Dr A.P.J. Abdul Kalam further inspired me to dream big. These two books taught me that personal dreams can become reality when pursued with clarity and intention.

During a brief stay in the United States, I discovered The Art of Living and learned Sudarshan Kriya, a powerful breathing technique for emotional balance. But the real transformation came after returning to India, through Landmark Education. The Landmark Forum changed how I viewed the world. One powerful insight: life is "empty and meaningless"—and we are the ones who give it meaning. This simple truth taught me that we have the power to author our own lives.

I joined the Landmark Assisting Programme, gaining hands-on experience in leadership and self-awareness. My journey continued through the Advanced Course, Seminar Series, and the Self-Expression and Leadership Programme, culminating in two years in the Course Supervisor Programme. These experiences honed my ability to listen deeply, hold space for transformation, and understand how language and context shape experience.

Exploring the work of Werner Erhard gave me a deeper grasp of transformation and the self. His book Transformation of a Man became a personal favourite. I also attended the Being a Leader programme, which deepened my understanding of ontological leadership. My interest in philosophy led me to briefly explore thinkers like Martin Heidegger and Bertrand Russell. While I didn't pursue it academically, these ideas expanded my understanding of leadership and human nature.

Yoga became a formal part of my life through a teacher training programme, helping me connect physical well-being with deeper reflection. Studying Patanjali's Yoga Sutras and the practical wisdom of Jeevan Vidya and H. Nagaraja helped me better understand life and relationships.

Eastern wisdom traditions have profoundly shaped my journey. The teachings of Buddhism, Zen, Osho, and J. Krishnamurti encouraged me to question patterns of thought and explore consciousness. Vedanta, especially through Swami Sarvapriyananda, added both spiritual and intellectual depth. My ongoing study of the Bhagavad Gita continues to offer timeless insights into life and self-awareness.

Design and typography have always fascinated me. My first exposure was with Aldus PageMaker on a Macintosh during school. The elegance of fonts captivated me and later led to calligraphy. I learned Adobe InDesign to format this book, and I hope to learn font design next. I believe good design can powerfully shape communication and perception.

In 2015, I moved from Bengaluru to London to launch ProcessWhirl. Adapting to a new culture and the challenges of entrepreneurship was both humbling and transformative. During this time, Siddhartha by Hermann Hesse became a companion—its message of self-discovery mirrored my own unfolding journey.

I've pursued many courses and earned multiple qualifications, including a Diploma in Law focused on Intellectual Property Rights. I also hold professional certifications, such as the PCC credential from the International Coaching Federation (ICF) and several Agile certifications. Learning has always brought me joy—long before the term 'lifelong learner' became fashionable.

The Oxford School of Hinduism and the London School of Philosophy and Economics further nurtured my curiosity, especially around the foundations of ethics.

Books, conversations, and everyday moments continue to shape my thinking. Sapiens, Autobiography of a Yogi, and the lives of Steve Jobs and Jack Ma taught me about innovation and resilience. Pixar's storytelling, Tony Robbins' tools, and design thinking have all influenced my views on creativity and impact.

Books and courses by Luc De Brabandere of BCG expanded my ability to think creatively and independently. Yvon Chouinard, founder of Patagonia, inspired me with his ethical, sustainable approach to business. Dr Promod Verma, architect of India's Aadhaar project, showed me how to design for scale. And Sridhar Vembu of Zoho, with whom I recorded my very first podcast, remains a personal inspiration.

Photography has been a passion since childhood. During COVID, I began sharing my photos for free. My Unsplash collection has since been viewed over two million times and is used by creative teams across the world.

Some of the most powerful learning has come from informal moments—conversations over coffee, long walks in London, and quiet reflection. The influence of mentors, friends, and chance encounters has been invaluable.

Design still inspires me—not just visually, but in how structure and clarity elevate expression. Whether leading a session or formatting a book, everything I've done has centred on one core goal: enabling transformation. Real change, I've found, doesn't come from knowing more—it comes from seeing differently.

A part of me will always be that curious boy from the village, drawn to paradox, possibility, and questions with no easy answers. Today, that same part of me stands ready to serve—supporting others as they find their own path forward.

WHAT NEXT is a programme born from a decade of discovery, experimentation, and human stories. It exists as more than a course—it's a mission-driven space where people reconnect with purpose, design meaningful lives, and take bold, conscious action. We are committed to making this work widely accessible so that individuals from all walks of life have the opportunity to explore what's next for them—with clarity, courage, and community.

Leading this next chapter is not a solo journey. I'm uplifted by the unwavering support of family and friends who continue to stand by me. We're building a core team—a circle of dedicated individuals who share a deep belief in transformation through community. United by purpose, we are committed to supporting others in living lives rooted in integrity, courage, and meaningful contribution.

Over the years, I've realised that frameworks and tools are useful—but what people remember most is how we make them feel. This journey is about presence, deep listening, and the courage to walk alongside one another.

Victories don't always come with trophies or titles. Sometimes, they show up as clarity, silence, or the strength to speak your truth. My definition of success now includes stillness, wonder, and joy.

Each moment, each failure, each lesson, and each experience has shaped who I am—a seeker, a creator, a coach, and a companion. The road hasn't always been easy, but it's been beautifully real.

Your journey is uniquely yours. If you're standing at a crossroads, wondering what's next, know this: the path ahead doesn't need to be clear for you to begin. Your story is unfolding in its own beautiful way. Your questions are welcome, your dreams are valid, and transformation begins the moment you choose to listen to that quiet voice within.

Openness to possibility is where it all begins. When we live in alignment with our purpose, grounded in values and supported by a caring community, so much more becomes possible. I believe in people. I believe in the strength, wisdom, and courage that live in each of us.

Understanding that you don't have to have it all figured out is freeing. You only need to take the next step. Wherever you are right now is a powerful place to begin—and I'll do my best to support you on this journey. Feel free to reach out to me at: mithare@explorewhatnext.com

SPECIAL THANKS TO

PAUL DRANAL

NATASHA CAUSTON

SVEN IHNKEN

SAVITH SR

RAJKUMAR NOUBADE

SUBODH KOPARDE

SHRIKANT HALANAYAK

NICK PERRY

"In today's rapidly evolving world—where technological advances and societal shifts are constantly redefining purpose and success—clarity of purpose has never been more essential for achieving true fulfilment. As we navigate the uncertainties of a changing world and seek to understand our place within it, the responsibility to define our own path and measures of success falls squarely on each of us.

This book presents a transformative framework, enriched with powerful tools and techniques, to support you on your journey of self-discovery. Through a clear and practical roadmap, Raghav empowers readers to take ownership of their lives, uncover their true purpose, and create a future aligned with their deepest values and aspirations."

> DEEPAK MALHOTRA, PARTNER, INFOSYS CONSULTING, UK

"As a coach, I often work with clients at pivotal moments—navigating mid-life transitions, career dilemmas, and the ever-present question: 'What next?' Raghavendra Mithare's book is a masterful guide that not only acknowledges this uncertainty but provides a structured, actionable roadmap to move from confusion to clarity. Drawing from powerful frameworks like the Hero's Journey, Ikigai, the Kübler-Ross Grief Curve, and the GQC (Goal-Question-Context) framework, this book equips readers with the tools to redesign their lives with purpose and intention.

Raghav weaves together personal insights, psychological principles, and real-world strategies to help individuals align their actions with their values, set meaningful goals, and navigate change with confidence. Whether it's embracing Vector Thinking to align direction and action, applying the Life Design Canvas to craft a fulfilling career, or reframing setbacks using lessons from resilience and mindset research, WHAT NEXT is more than just a book—it's a coaching conversation in itself.

I highly recommend this book to coaches, mentors, and leaders who seek a transformative resource for their coachees and mentees. It's the perfect gift for anyone ready to step beyond uncertainty and actively design the life they truly deserve."

BHASKAR NATARAJAN, MCC (ICF), EXECUTIVE, LEADERSHIP AND CXO COACH, BENGALURU, INDIA

What Next by Raghavendra Mithare is a truly inspiring and well-structured guide that delves into self-discovery, purpose, and personal growth. He brings his rich experience and wisdom, along with real-world success stories, into a practical framework. The book is well-organised and thoroughly researched; drawing on a range of sources, it offers various models to help you realise new perspectives and ideas. I truly believe that anyone who wishes to build a life with clarity and purpose must read this book.

MANIKANTH L B, CO-FOUNDER, DIRECTOR-LUCID | SALES & MARKETING | MOTIVATOR | SPEAKER | FITNESS PRACTITIONER | BLOGGER

I've known Raghav for over a decade, and one thing that has always stood out about him is his deeply reflective nature. He's not someone who just skims the surface of life—he dives in, questioning, exploring, and unpacking the layers beneath everyday experiences. It's not brooding—it's a thoughtful curiosity that leads him to see life through a unique lens. You could say he wears a special pair of glasses—ones with a bit of x-ray vision that allow him to notice what most of us might overlook. This book is a natural outcome of that superpower. It's a culmination of the insights he has gathered over years of observation, reflection, and personal growth.
At its core, the book is a guided journey into self-discovery,

centred around the quest to live a life of purpose. In this book, Raghav doesn't preach—he invites. He nudges the reader to explore the 'why,' 'how,' and 'when' of living meaningfully. Throughout the book, you'll find glimpses of that same thoughtful lens he wears—how he draws lessons from everyday moments and distils them into simple, actionable insights.

What makes this book especially impactful is how grounded it is. It's not just theory—it's full of practical exercises and reflections that help the reader engage actively with their own journey. If you are looking for a companion to help you explore life with clarity, this book is a great place to start.

HARI SRINIVASAN, CHIEF EXECUTIVE OFFICER
AT GARBHAGUDI INSTITUTE OF REPRODUCTIVE
HEALTH AND RESEARCH

WHAT NEXT by Raghavendra Mithare is a powerful and thought-provoking self-help book that challenges readers to break free from the limiting beliefs shaped by upbringing and societal norms. With clarity and conviction, Mithare emphasizes the importance of mental liberation as the foundation for personal transformation. He makes a compelling case that wealth is not merely material but deeply rooted in one's mindset—"think rich to be rich" becomes more than a slogan; it's a call to action. The book dives into how individuals perceive money differently and encourages readers to reprogram their thoughts for abundance. Equally important is his message on time management—Mithare illustrates how mastering one's hours is key to mastering one's life. His writing is grounded in extensive research and filled with practical insights that readers can apply immediately. The tone is encouraging yet firm, making the book both a motivational push and a guidebook for self-discipline. Mithare's wisdom flows with simplicity and force, making each page feel like a conversation with a mentor. What Next? is not just another self-help read; it's a million-dollar mindset shift waiting to happen.

SUBODH KOPARDE, ENTERPRISE ARCHITECT,
THOUGHT LEADER, WASHINGTON DC, USA.

Follow on Instagram

@EXPLOREWHATNEXT

BUY FROM BYSTANDER

Ships within UK only

www.ingramcontent.com/pod-product-compliance
Lightning Source LLC
Chambersburg PA
CBHW020340010526
44119CB00048B/540